Washington inherited his first slave at age eleven, and throughout his life, he was seldom far from enslaved African Americans until his death on December 14, 1799.

Slavery

AT THE HOME OF GEORGE WASHINGTON

Edited by
Philip J. Schwarz

Jean B. Lee   Edna Greene Medford

Dennis J. Pogue   James C. Rees

Mary V. Thompson   Lorena S. Walsh

This publication was made possible by
a generous grant from
The Honorable and Mrs. Togo D. West, Jr.

Mount Vernon Ladies' Association
Mount Vernon, Virginia 22121

The Mount Vernon Ladies' Association
P.O. Box 110
Mount Vernon, VA 22191
www.mountvernon.org

ISBN   0-931917-

Photographs: Larry Olson, 21; Dennis Pogue, 33, 110, 114, 124;
James Rees, 46, 56, 58; Ed Owen, 98, 126; Paul Kennedy, 117;
Michael Quinn, 121; Mark Finkenstaedt, 60, 142, 145, 146, 171;
Robert C. Lautman, 167, 168; Roy Karten, 173

TABLE OF CONTENTS

The scene depicted in this 19th-century print shows slaves and members of the plantation owner's family living different lives, but in harmony with each other. The pages that follow will shed light on the accuracy of this depiction.

INTRODUCTION
PHILIP J. SCHWARZ

Until recently historians have mostly ignored a role George Washington played through much of his lifetime. Washington the planter, Washington the patriot, Washington the general, and Washington the president loom large, but, once recognized, so does Washington the slave owner. Mr. Washington may have spent more of his lifetime overseeing enslaved laborers than he did supervising soldiers or government officials. And well he might because under his direction those slaves produced the wealth that he enjoyed and that helped him become a leader in Virginia and later in the United States.

The popular view many people hold of George Washington has changed in recent years because of increased attention to African-American history. Many people simply wish to know more about how Washington interacted with the Mount Vernon slave population. Historians also study how colonial and early national black people interacted with white people. They ask how Washington's human property lived in bondage to Washington. Visitors to Mount Vernon have increasingly asked about African-American life there. Conscious of this new interest and of the burgeoning scholarship on slavery, to which Mount Vernon Ladies' Association personnel have contributed, the Association (with the support of the W. K. Kellogg Foundation) held a conference on "Slavery in the Age of Washington" in November 1994. The essays in this volume are based on presentations made at that well-attended conference. It is hoped that these essays will answer some of the questions Mount Vernon visitors have posed as well as encourage more questions and research.

GEORGE WASHINGTON'S AND VIRGINIA'S INHERITANCE

George Washington's career as a planter represents a very profitable outcome of the social and economic system into which he was born in 1732. While Washington acquired the basis for his wealth by inheritance and marriage, he also acquired and inherited widely held assumptions about how to acquire and develop even more wealth. Besides the agricultural and trading practices that had stood the test of time, Virginia's and Maryland's labor system was the means a free white plantation owner would employ to seek either solvency or wealth. Slavery was the traditional, mostly unquestioned labor system of all the southern colonies and of areas in several northern colonies by 1760. Virginia had the largest enslaved population in the North American colonies (ca. 140,000).

The supply and control of labor were crucial factors in 17th-century Virginia's economic development. Large landowners then grew tobacco using white servile labor. The supply and control of labor were still important in the 18th century, except that the laboring people were now enslaved Africans and their descendants. The labor system was now racial slavery. The white supremacist assumptions of the post-1700 social, economic, and labor system of Virginia made all the difference. Virginia had become a slave society by the 1700s and very few white people of the time had raised any public objection to that transformation.

Labor supply and labor control were always essential to the transformation of Virginia. If either was weak, the economic and social gains some Virginians had already enjoyed could turn to dust. By the last few decades of the 17th century, the supply of European servants declined; and therefore servants became more expensive. Planters were also less confident about controlling these laborers. The supply of enslaved Africans increased during the late 1600s, so their price decreased. The race was on for British slave traders to supply enslaved laborers and for Chesapeake planters to buy them. White planters were also confident they could control Africans. By 1760, when George Washington's quest to improve Mount Vernon began, he inherited or gained control over slaves whom other people had bought from traders or who had been born in North America or the West Indies to Africans and African Americans. For a time Washington also bought slave labor. As a result, the enslaved Mount Vernon community had diverse roots. It is no wonder that they did; between 1700 and 1789 far more Africans crossed the Atlantic to the Chesapeake than did Europeans.[1]

Enslaved labor was anything but static, though. In 1760, about

17 percent of the income-producing (tithable) Virginian slaves worked in the seven counties in which George Washington owned or controlled land after he married Martha Dandridge Custis. By 1800, however, the 30,000 enslaved people (including non-income-producing children and others) in the same counties as those mentioned above constituted only about nine percent of the Old Dominion's slave population. The "center of gravity" of slavery in 1760 had shifted to southside and piedmont Virginia. That shift occurred because Chesapeake planters like Washington decided to de-emphasize tobacco and to give new and increasing attention to corn and grain.

When the Chesapeake's King Tobacco retreated from the area, George Washington and other planters had to adjust their labor needs. Some planters decided that they had too many slaves to manage the less labor-intensive grain and corn crops. Surplus labor would cut into profits. So those planters cut their losses by selling the "excess" slaves to southern Virginia, Kentucky and other expanding territories and states. (Later sales would be to the cotton and sugar states.) Washington thought otherwise. He planned for Mount Vernon's enslaved laborers to do new kinds of work as described by Jean Lee's and Lorena Walsh's essays. And the essays by Mary Thompson, Dennis Pogue, and Edna Greene Medford show that those workers made decisions about their own lives that sometimes clashed with Washington's plans. Like any community, Mount Vernon encompassed divergent points of view that should be recognized.

New Perceptions

Hierarchical and sometimes racist perceptions have obscured our understanding of the Mount Vernon community. George Washington has loomed largest, as befits his accomplishments. But Martha Washington has sometimes been a very distant second and, with the exception of Billy Lee and West Ford, most Africans and African Americans at Mount Vernon have been all but invisible. The essays in this volume reflect an improved perception of the labor, skills, families, private lives, and even descendants of black Mount Vernon.

The essays that follow also integrate consideration of Washington, Mount Vernon, African Americans under Washington's control, and regional or national circumstances. Both Jean Lee and Lorena Walsh make clear the extent to which Washington planned almost every activity on his real property as well as the ways enslaved laborers, whom he also regarded as his personal property, mastered some very complex agricultural tasks but also sometimes resisted Washington's plans. Thus Washington, who had few problems with the labor supply at Mount Vernon, had several kinds of control problems with the human beings who had their own ideas about their role on the estate.

WASHINGTON'S PLAN

Because George Washington's plans for his plantation's growth affected so much of the Mount Vernon slaves' lives, Jean Lee's essay appropriately begins this volume. "Mount Vernon Plantation: A Model for the Republic" makes clear Washington's objectives: systematization, innovation, and improvement. While Washington worked regularly and very diligently to reach these objectives, the plantation's enslaved labor force had some difficulty internalizing Washington's plans. When an observer pointed out that overseers of Washington's farms and slaves might be called generals at the head of a system, he perfectly captured how General Washington required order and system, including frequent and detailed reports from his overseers, as part of his overall plan. And the overseers no doubt ordered the plantation workers to complete their tasks in a manner that would make excellent reports possible.

But by the 1780s, General Washington generally did not rule with a heavy hand. As Jean Lee makes clear, Washington increasingly rejected the traditional means of coercing his slaves. He turned against selling recalcitrant slaves "at public auction," something he had done before. He developed a conscience, or at least a consciousness, of enslaved people's feelings about punitive family separation. And he even told his supervisors to put their whips away. What results did Washington gain from this relatively innovative approach to slave labor? "Where he wanted order and perfection,"

Ms. Lee concludes, "the laborers seem to have been satisfied with sufficiency and minimal exertion." Washington would finally conclude that Mount Vernon would not become "a model for the republic" because it was impossible to solve the several problems he encountered, not the least of which was the unwillingness of his human property to internalize his objectives and principles.

AGRICULTURE AND SLAVERY

However, Lorena Walsh's essay, "Slavery and Agriculture at Mount Vernon," reveals evidence of success in the Mount Vernon labor force's efforts. The Mount Vernon "men, women, and children employed the knowledge and skills they possessed," she argues, "to further the productive goals of the estate, to maintain their families and improve their living conditions, and to resist the strenuous demands that Washington tried to impose." Ms. Walsh's perception of the laborers' motives gives them their due. They may not have adopted Washington's vision of Mount Vernon as a "model for the republic" as their own, but they did have clear goals for themselves just as Washington did for himself. And Lorena Walsh's rigorous explanation of the complex agricultural techniques Washington demanded and that enslaved laborers mastered encourages respect for their work in spite of Washington's disappointment and pessimism.

"Slavery and Agriculture at Mount Vernon" focuses not only on the "innovative labor management strategies" necessitated by Washington's vision for his plantation, but also on the complex and far-reaching changes the enslaved labor force at Mount Vernon had to effect. According to Walsh, "Mount Vernon's enslaved laborers became some of the most skilled mixed-crop farmers, fishermen, and stock breeders in the region." Thus the "sufficiency and minimal exertion" to which Jean Lee refers was in fact enough to increase the skills of Mount Vernon's agricultural workers. Ms. Walsh's detailed knowledge of 18th-century Chesapeake area agriculture leaves a strong impression not only of the difficulties Washington and the Mount Vernon labor force faced but, more importantly, also the relative success they achieved. To be sure, Washington deserves much of the credit for their relative success. But the Walsh essay paints a vivid picture of the Mount Vernon men and women working with Washington a good deal of the time to understand and employ those innovative techniques and unfamiliar crops they regarded as worthwhile.

Washington did develop some innovative labor management techniques. He placed people with compatible abilities and knowledge into the same work groups; he appointed some black overseers; he negotiated new "customs of the plantations"; and he sometimes responded positively to complaints about insufficient rations once he received credible evidence of the insufficiency. But Walsh concludes that ultimately the Mount Vernon people "had ample reason for failing to respond enthusiastically to Washington's demand that they sacrifice what little leisure time they could command for the betterment of a new nation in which they had no personal stake."

Free Time

Mary Thompson's essay concentrates on the leisure time the slaves were unwilling to sacrifice. Ms. Thompson's essay, "'They Appear to Live Comfortable Together': Private Lives of the Mount Vernon Slaves," shows what made leisure time so important to enslaved Mount Vernon people.

While not legally protected, enslaved Africans and African Americans clearly placed a high value on marriage. Still, some spouses had to live apart because they did not live on the same farm. Children from plantation marriages helped swell the Mount Vernon population from approximately 50 in 1759 to more than 300 at the time of Washington's death. They also extended intergenerational connections and spread inherited knowledge. Ms. Thompson makes clear that slave births were accorded some protection by either black or white midwives and that parents appear to have been able to choose names for their newborn children on their own. Thompson's essay sheds much light on enslaved children's play as well. But the children would still eventually become "working boys and girls," thereby entering an informal apprenticeship for later work.

Free time could be productive as well as leisure time. Mount

Vernon workers could use free time to "benefit themselves and their families, rather than their master." Self-education occurred during time off as did money making enterprises. But free time was equally valued as an opportunity to visit, enjoy music, smoke pipes, play games such as prisoner's base, swim in the Potomac, tell stories, or attend horse races in Alexandria. Religion was important to some enslaved Mount Vernon workers. A handful of slaves may have been preachers; others may have practiced African religions. As for last things, slaves were obviously allowed to bury their loved ones.

The most important implication of Ms. Thompson's essay is that the private lives of African Americans at Mount Vernon demonstrate their ability to live at times according to their own values even though Washington had the power to intervene in those lives at any time.

UNDERGROUND MOUNT VERNON

As all the essayists acknowledge, there are aspects of the relationship between George Washington and the enslaved people of Mount Vernon, as well as of the private lives of those subordinated people, that still are obscure or hidden. Dennis Pogue, who has become an expert on the physical underside of today's Mount Vernon, has teased out aspects of "Slave Lifeways at Mount Vernon" from archaeological evidence. Without his having discovered the remains of slave life, we would have missed important aspects of their working and private lives.

Fortunately for us, it is as if George Washington had arranged for an excellent site from which archaeologists could gather evidence of slaves' material culture. Washington directed the construction of a House for Families, meaning slave families, that was almost 4,000 square feet in size. This house stood until the winter of 1792-93, and therefore represents the remains of a living space inhabited by a significant number of enslaved Mount Vernon people. One could say that while historians read other people's mail, archaeologists go through other people's trash. And it is the trash that was disposed of beneath the house that now speaks to us from two centuries ago.

Dr. Pogue and his fellow archaeologists discovered material

objects in the trash receptacle that could have been found in a relatively prosperous planter's house. Yet there are unmistakable artifacts of an African or African-American cultural origin. Only a biologist or anatomist might love one such object. A raccoon baculum (penis bone) could be an utterly prosaic item to be inventoried and forgotten. But Pogue and his colleagues noticed that someone had modified the bone "by incising a line encircling one end." Was it a fertility symbol suspended around one's neck? If so, was it a distinctively African symbol?

The quality of other artifacts in the trash indicates the higher status of the Mansion House slaves who lived in the House for Families. Dishes and similar objects might have been used in the Mansion House and then handed down to the people in the House for Families. The nature of some other artifacts is abundantly clear because they were used in particular occupations. And there are numerous objects that may have been used as jewelry or adornment. One can even infer the types of meals slaves ate from the kinds of bowls they used.

Dr. Pogue acknowledges that finds from the House for Families dig cannot be used as evidence of all slave life at Mount Vernon. But for now it is possible to conclude that slaves lived "a less controlled existence" at Mount Vernon than a "stereotypical view of slavery" might lead one to believe. And the dig of a Mount Vernon slave site has also raised as many questions as it has answered. For example, did slaves hunt and fish to diversify their food supply; or did Washington and his overseers provide inadequate food?

MOUNT VERNON DESCENDANTS

Family histories may provide more evidence about life at Washington's Mount Vernon. Given the presence of about three hundred enslaved African Americans at Mount Vernon at the time of George Washington's death in 1799, the number of their descendants must be quite large by now. Thanks to the efforts of such bodies as the Quanders United Incorporated and the Gum Springs Historical Society, memories of several families have been actively preserved. Edna Greene Medford's essay, "Beyond Mount

Vernon: George Washington's Emancipated Laborers and Their Descendants," gives more attention to those descendants who have appeared in published accounts. Surely others will be discussed as time goes by.

Freedom for slaves was the appropriate coda to George Washington's life, but Ms. Medford makes clear that the freedom he granted to his enslaved laborers in his will was limited by the white-supremacist society in which these people would live and also by a crucial circumstance of the Mount Vernon population. Washington owned only some of the people who labored for him. So George Washington freed all his slaves, but he could not free the entire enslaved population of Mount Vernon.

Edna Medford's essay follows the manner in which some former Mount Vernon people struggled with their legacy and with their new lives in a society that regarded them as anomalous and suspect because they contradicted the assumed enslavement of all black people. Fortunately some laws protected aspects of these people's freedom. The law that required each free person of color to register with public authorities identified free people not only to their contemporaries but also to historians. Ms. Medford makes full use of the Alexandria and Fairfax County registers to follow the lives of former Mount Vernon slaves. The registers are a gold mine concerning many people. In a sense, George Washington's conferral of freedom upon his slaves also gave us the gift of good information about some of them.

Ms. Medford indicates that many of the freedpeople and their children remained in the Mount Vernon area. Some of the manumitted people stayed at Mount Vernon to take advantage of the financial support provisions required by Virginia's manumission law. Other former Washington slaves maintained some kind of association with their original home plantation. These two groups of people were well represented in area church and other leadership positions and some were able to attain a level of prosperity. Further research will undoubtedly augment our historical knowledge of people formerly enslaved at Mount Vernon.

This 18th-century engraving by Jacques Le Roy after John Trumbull shows Washington as the lean and commanding military leader, but it also reflects that a slave was often by his side during the military years, as well as his years at Mount Vernon.

UNFINISHED BUSINESS

Historical research never ends. New evidence appears, and different generations find new meanings. The essays in this volume reflect contemporary understandings of George Washington and slavery. Henry Wiencek, author of *The Hairstons: an American Family in Black and White*, is writing a study of Washington and his enslaved workers. Other work is in progress. One can tell from the questions some of these essayists have asked, their silences about certain matters, disagreements among authors, and the state of contemporary research that the study of slavery and George Washington, this relatively new topic, will continue. We need to know much more about the specific African and American origins of Washington's workers, which Lorena Walsh discussed in her essay, as well as about the individuals who comprised the field labor force under Washington's control. Perhaps oral history like the "Getting Word" project at Thomas Jefferson's Monticello will glean valuable family stories from descendants of the African-American Mount Vernon people. Jean Lee's forthcoming book on George Washington and Lorena Walsh's study in progress concerning Chesapeake agriculture will answer some more questions, as will the ongoing research by Dennis Pogue and Mary Thompson at Mount Vernon. But the research is in full swing and the authors of these essays have given you a full taste of its current results.

NOTES

1 Philip D. Morgan, *Slave Counterpoint: Black Culture in the Eighteenth-Century Chesapeake and Lowcountry* (Chapel Hill, 1998), xv.

A Division of the Negro's made, and agreed to between Col.º George Lee, and the Brothers of the deceas'd Maj.ʳ Lawrence Washington, the 10ᵗʰ day of December Anno Domini 1754 ——

Col.º Lee's part		The Estates part	
Old Moll	£25	Phebe	£25
Lawrence	60	Peter	60
Ben	40	Pharro	40
Will	40	Abram	40
Frank	40	Couta	40
Barbara	40	Nell	40
Moll	25	Jate	25
Milly	20	Betta	20
Hannah	15	Barbara	15
Penny	10	Anteno	10
Will	10	Dier at Sando	10
Nan	15	Aaron	15
Nan	31	Judah	25
James	40	Ned	40
Jula	40	Cameo	40
Dublin	40	Jambo	40
Acco	40	Jando	40
Harry	35	Scipio	25
Roger	40	Tomboy	40
Grace	40	Salt	40
Phillis	40	Jenny	40
Kate	40	Judah	40
Cæsar	25	Tom	15
Farro	1 M.ᵗʰ Old	Phil	
Charles	2.7½	Tom	4.1
Doll	3.4	Prince	3.7½
Sue	2.11½	Belly	2.1
George	3.7½	Lucy	4.1
Lydia	2.5½	Sam	2.9
Jenn	5 M.ᵗʰ Old	Tom	4 M.ᵗʰ Old
Haggon		Joey	1 M.ᵗʰ Old

This slave census of December 10, 1754, reveals the division of slaves of the deceased Lawrence Washington, George Washington's elder half-brother.

12

Mount Vernon Plantation: A Model For The Republic

Jean B. Lee

I n Colonel Landon Carter's famous plantation diary (1752-78), he recorded a quarter-century's efforts to analyze, order, and rationalize his land and laborers at Sabine Hall, his Virginia tidewater plantation. In addition to experimenting with crops and crop rotation to maximize yields, Carter designed a mathematically exact cornfield, with every cornstalk precisely positioned in relation to all the others, and conducted time studies of slaves' work so that their productivity might be increased. "This world," he believed, "has somehow been established upon the principles of number, weight, and measure."[1]

Other Virginians, including George Washington, also sought to systematize their operations, often under the influence of English agricultural innovations. For example, two miles up the Rappahannock River from Carter's Sabine Hall, John Tayloe III began managing Mount Airy plantation in the 1790s and soon became a highly successful Chesapeake entrepreneur. He ran a mostly self-sufficient estate by utilizing 40 percent of his slaves as artisans and domestics, and optimized profits by maintaining a disproportionately male labor force. After European tobacco markets collapsed during the Napoleonic wars, Tayloe concentrated on large-scale grain production. By 1809, some two hundred plows turned the soil at Mount Airy, soil that was yielding eight to ten thousand bushels of wheat and about five thousand barrels of corn annually.[2]

A hundred miles to the west, where the rolling hills of the piedmont meet the Blue Ridge mountains, Thomas Jefferson methodically recorded daily weather conditions and plantation activities at Monticello. Aiming to improve his estate and income, and styling himself "the most ardent farmer in the state," he established a profitable nailery that supplied his own and nearby planters' needs, invented a moldboard for a plow, and bought the most modern machinery available for his grain operations. A visitor to Monticello in 1796 found Jefferson "employed with activity and perseverance in the management of his farms and buildings . . . he orders, directs, and pursues in the minutest detail every branch of business relative to them."[3]

The adult lives of these Virginian plantation owners spanned the last half of the 18th century and the first quarter of the 19th. Their goals for their estates, the time they actually spent in residence, and their management styles varied, sometimes markedly. Yet, what figuratively united them, and distinguished them from many other planters, was their devotion to ideas and methods commonly associated with the Scientific Revolution and the Enlightenment: a passion for experimentation, fascination with machinery and numbers, dedication to order and rationality, and to improvement and progress, and commitment to meticulous record-keeping so that experiments, observations, and progress could be duly noted. In their preoccupation with managing productive processes and their laborers, these Virginians had much in common with northern mill and factory owners of the 19th century. No one more fully fits these generalizations than George Washington.

Washington began his years at Mount Vernon not as an innovative, enlightened farmer but as a traditional Chesapeake tobacco planter, intent upon expanding his holdings of land and slaves and dependent upon the London consignment trade.[4] Then, during a tenure of more than four decades on his ancestral estate, he was instrumental in transforming its architecture, landscape, and economy. In the process he also transformed himself into a scientific, experimental, visionary farmer. By the 1780s, no American of his generation was more passionately dedicated to agricultural innovation and improvement or to creating a well ordered landscape and labor force.

The architectural and landscape design of Mount Vernon gradually changed from the utilitarian, rustic plantation built by Washington's father and half-brother to the orderly country estate sketched by Samuel Vaughan in 1787. The plan of the estate successfully adapted British styles, both in the more or less symmetrical placement of buildings, gardens, serpentine walks, and undulating ha-has and in the clear demarcation of borders between carefully contoured and tended grounds and, beyond them, natural woodlands and the Potomac River. Noted a European traveler in 1798, "The G[enera]l has never left America. After seeing his house and his gardens one would say that he had seen the most beautiful examples in England of this style." Yet Mount Vernon's architecture also was quintessentially Virginian, for it replicated spatially the hierarchical social order of the 18th-century Chesapeake. By the 1790s anyone walking from the general's house southward toward the river landing passed, in succession, the kitchen, overseer's quarters, smokehouse, washhouse, coachhouse, and stable. Setting out in the opposite, northerly direction from the Mansion House, one passed the farm manager's and gardener's residences, a salt house, spinning house, and finally, slave quarters that faced outward, away from the carefully arranged gardens, walkways, and grounds. The structures for slaves and livestock — positioned farthest architecturally and socially from the Mansion House — balanced one another schematically on opposite sides of the compound.[5]

No less dramatically, Washington transformed the plantation's economy, beginning in the 1760s. The title of a volume in his library, *A New System of Agriculture: Or a Speedy Method of Growing Rich*, was

This 1792 painting of Mount Vernon, attributed to Edward Savage, shows the House for Families, which Washington later removed from the North Lane.

G. Washington

ESSAYS AND NOTES

ON

HUSBANDRY

AND

RURAL AFFAIRS.

By J. B. BORDLEY.

Still let me COUNTRY CULTURE fcan :
My FARM's my Home : " My Brother, MAN :
" And GOD is every where."

PHILADELPHIA :

PRINTED BY BUDD AND BARTRAM,

FOR THOMAS DOBSON, AT THE STONE HOUSE,

No 41, SOUTH SECOND STREET.

1799.

In all likelihood, Bordley's Essays and Notes on Husbandry and Rural Affairs *was one of Washington's favorite books in his library.*

emblematic of the metamorphosis underway. Unsatisfied with his returns in the tobacco trade, he decided to abandon tobacco cultivation altogether, converted to commercial grain production, and eventually experimented with about sixty different crops. Determined to free himself from dependence on the consignment trade, he became involved with grain voyages to the West Indies, established a weaving operation using homespun flax, and added to the estate's commercial activities with a ferry, fishery, and gristmill. Colonial resistance to the Stamp Act and the Townshend Duties spurred his conversion to grain production and greater plantation self-sufficiency.[6]

Notwithstanding the innovations instituted at Mount Vernon during the colonial period, Washington did nothing to change the traditional slave labor system. He began farming with African-Americans whom he had inherited, more than doubled his labor force with the dower slaves that Martha Dandridge Custis brought to their marriage, and occasionally purchased additional laborers, including a few Africans. Natural increase also added to the plantation's black population, which grew to about 135 people by 1774. Like most white southerners, Washington seems not to have questioned the institution of human bondage. Labor was a commodity, a "species of property," and he spoke of his slaves in distant, impersonal terms. Moreover, he willingly used harsh discipline in retribution for behavior he considered unacceptable and as a warning to all of his chattel. The crack of the whip reverberated across the fields and quarters, and Washington did not hesitate to dispatch a "Rogue & Runaway" to the West Indies, thereby dooming the man to a notoriously brutal slave regime and also permanently removing him from whatever family and friends he may have had in Virginia. During the colonial period, therefore, change at the plantation proceeded with an ancient and servile labor system.[7]

The American Revolution vastly amplified and gave new meaning and purpose — a civic purpose — to Washington's penchant for improving Mount Vernon. To many of his generation, the Revolution assumed transcendent importance. It had no parallels in human history, thought James Madison, and it harbored "lessons of which prosperity ought not to be deprived." Some conceived of the new United States as a laboratory of the Enlightenment, the best place on earth where ideals of human progress and perfectibility might be realized. Fortunately, said Washington, the nation was not founded "in the gloomy age of Ignorance and Superstition." An exemplar of the practical, utilitarian side of the Enlightenment — "the pursuit of useful knowledge," as he phrased it — he hoped to make Mount Vernon a model plantation, one that would instruct and inspire the citizenry of the entire nation in habits he deemed essential for the republic. Mount Vernon would be a paragon of order, efficiency, industriousness, productivity, and self-sufficiency. Therefore, after returning home from the Continental Army in 1783, Washington devoted a tremendous amount of his own time and energy, and that of his labor force, to perfecting his estate aesthetically and to experimenting with the most advanced agricultural techniques of his day. These preoccupations are linked symbolically in the decor of the grandest room in his house, the two-story dining room whose "richly ornamented" plaster ceiling is embossed with a sheaf of wheat, a scythe, a plow, and other agricultural implements.[8]

In these endeavors Washington was exhibiting what he once called "the investigating geniu[s of] the present age" or, to phrase it another way, the passion of the American Revolutionary generation to improve everything from constitutions to human nature itself. He also was driven by his own proclivity for order and regularity, for, he believed, "to establish good rules, and a regular system, is the life, and the soul of every kind of business." A visitor who in 1787 found Mount Vernon "the most charming Seat I have seen in America," reported that it "is kept with great Neatness[,] & the good Order of the Masters Mind appears extended to every Thing around it." Furthermore, Washington's vision of his estate was part of a much larger vision of the Potomac River valley. If the river were made navigable almost to the headwaters of the Ohio River system, then the Potomac-Ohio route would become the most vital artery into the interior of the Continent. Millions of bushels of wheat and other agricultural products would be carried from the fresh lands and neat farms of the transmontane West to the market towns of Alexandria and Georgetown. A capital city befitting the republic would rise along the Maryland shore. And finally, a federal armory at Harper's Ferry, Virginia, and a fort sited just upriver from Mount Vernon would protect the capital and its hinterlands from hostile invasion. What better place could there be for the republic's model plantation?[9]

Transforming the ancestral Washington lands into an agriculturally advanced, aesthetically pleasing estate situated on "one of the finest rivers in the world" would require an enormous amount of manual labor. To provide it, Washington called upon his few white laborers and an enslaved African-American population that ranged from two hundred to over three hundred people between the mid-1780s and 1800.[10] In addition to their labor, he wanted from the men and women who inhabited Mount Vernon a level of industriousness that matched his own. Not surprisingly, the laboring hands did not necessarily embrace his work ethic or his plans; and

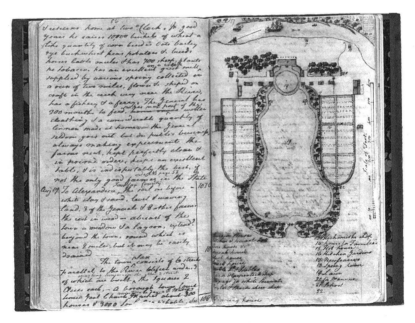

The journal kept by Englishman Samuel Vaughan during his visit to Mount Vernon is a detailed and artistic resource for scholars studying Washington's landscape and architecture. Vaughan commented that Washington was "always making experiments" in his agricultural pursuits.

ultimately Washington did not achieve the model plantation or labor force that he envisioned. His was a journey from ambitious plans to dissatisfaction and disillusionment.

To begin with the ambitious plans: after resigning his army commission, Washington returned home determined to be the Cincinnatus of Mount Vernon. "Under the shadow of my own Vine & my own Fig tree, free from the bustle of a camp & the busy scenes of public life," he told the Marquis de Lafayette, he would find solace in "tranquil enjoyments." Those enjoyments included supervising work on the buildings and grounds of the Mansion House Farm and, for all five farms comprising the Mount Vernon tract, a "new mode of cultivation." "Agriculture has ever been amongst the most favourite amusements of my life," he told the English agronomist Arthur Young in 1786, "though I never possessed much skill in the art." Now, with guidance from the published writings and personal correspondence of Young and other enlightened agronomists, Mount Vernon would have perfectly ordered fields and grounds, seeded with everything from timothy to burnet, from South Carolina palmetto plants and Georgia peaches to Russian wheat. Carefully conceived rotation of crops, plus application of manure and compost, would restore rather than exhaust the soil. To complete the pastoral scene, farm animals (including a superior breed of mules sired by a jackass from the royal stables of Spain) would power advanced plows, harrows, and other farm machinery. With this scheme Washington was consciously renouncing what he labeled the "ruinous" and "unproductive" practices of Chesapeake planters, "whose knowledge, [or] practice at least, centre in the destruction of the land, and very little beyond it," and who were "ever averse to novelty in matters of this sort, & much attached to their old customs." In 1785 he wrote, "it is my earnest wish to adopt a better . . . course of Husbandry."[11]

Raising his sights from the Potomac shores to the nation as a whole, Washington was convinced that the "welfare and prosperity" of the new republic depended upon agriculture and, therefore, that "a **course** of experiments by intelligent and observant farmers" was crucially important. "Every improvement in husbandry should be gratefully received and peculiarly fostered in this Country," not only

20

to forward the interests and reduce the labor of farmers, but also to advance "our respectability in a national point of view." Shortly after attending the Constitutional Convention of 1787, he told Jefferson that "the introduction of any thing which will divert our attention from Agriculture, must be extremely prejudicial, if not ruinous to us." About the same time, Washington ordered construction of a new barn, which a correspondent in New York pronounced "a true monument of Patriotism as it is intended to preserve the produce of a new mode of cultivation, which will greatly conduce to the happiness and prosperity of a people who are to form a nation." Small wonder, then, that the most revered man in America hoped to end his years as a "reputable" farmer.[12]

With so much seemingly at stake, Washington set out to organize, harmonize, perfect, and beautify everything in sight. Ground for new fields had to be cleared, broken, and tilled; old fields needed improvement. No field was to present "a grievous eye-sore." "Let the hands at the Mansion House Grub *well*, and

In the early 1790s, Washington built a 16-sided treading barn on his Dogue Run Farm.

perfectly prepare the old clover lot," he ordered. "When I say grub *well*, I mean that everything wch. is not to remain as trees should be taken up by the roots; so . . . that the Plow may meet with no interruption, and the field lye perfectly smooth for the Scythe. . . . I had rather have *one Acre* cleared in this manner, than four in the common mode." Such fields became the site of carefully planned "experiments," a word common in his references to agriculture. Employing the scientific method leading from observation to the acquisition of new knowledge, Washington planned, observed, and noted the amount of seed and fertilizer applied to the land, effects of plowing, weeding, and weather, the condition of plantings, and crop yields.[13]

Because growing crops needed protection from animals, and also for aesthetic reasons, the reputable farmer directed that miles of timbered and live fencing and ornamental borders were to be built, planted, or transplanted. "There is nothing I have so much at heart," he wrote, "as to introduce live fences around *every* Inclosure where Hogs are not suffered to be; and this is the case of all the inner Inclosures at the Mansion House, and division fences at the Plantations." No effort was spared on these projects. For example, after summer heat killed freshly transplanted trees beside the new serpentine walks, slaves were required to try again, in winter, and then to dig up each tree when the ground was frozen solid, and "with a large block of frozen earth" around the roots.[14]

Additional labor went into moving old buildings and constructing new ones. When the Mansion House gardens were redone, slave men dragged the old garden houses as much as 150 feet to new positions, as Washington noted in his diary in February 1786: "Having assembled the Men from my Plantations, I removed the garden Houses which were in the middle of the front walls to the extreme points of them; which were done with more ease, & less damage than I expected, considering the height one of them was to be raised from the ground." Even on the outlying farms, he was concerned with "the appearance of the place." In 1793, for example, he ordered the dwellings at Union Farm to be moved and lined up alongside a road. That configuration, he announced, "will be more

To construct his treading barn, Washington ordered 40,000 bricks, all to be made on the estate. These bricks were made in a similar fashion for the reconstruction of Washington's barn.

pleasing to me." Finally, in the early 1790s he decided to build a large 16-sided, brick-and-timber barn at Dogue Run Farm. On the long list of construction materials were 40 thousand bricks, all to be made on the plantation.[15]

To keep track of these and the other, unending tasks he assigned, Washington required the overseer of each of the farms to report to him once a week, even during his presidency. He wanted to know, in detail, what the domestic servants, seamstresses, spinners, gardeners, millers, coopers, carpenters, masons, wagoners, livestock handlers, drivers, and field hands had accomplished. It was as if — having spent eight years organizing and commanding an army — he could not break the habit, a point not lost on William Maclay, who noted in his diary that the overseers of the farms "may be stiled Generals — under Whom are Grades of Subordinate Appointments descending down thro Whites Mulattoes Negroes Horses Cows Sheep Hogs &ca. it was hinted that all were named. . . . Friday of every Week is appointed for the Overseers, or we will say Brigadier Generals[,] to make up their returns. not a days Work, but is noted What, by Whom, and Where done, not a Cow calves or Ewe drops her lamb, but is registered. deaths &ca. Whether accidental or by the hands of the Butcher, all minuted. Thus the etiquette and arrangement of an army is preserved on his farm."[16]

As thoroughly as any 19th-century factory owner (to change metaphors), Washington knew what he wanted from the people under his command and in his employ. His correspondence is replete with the qualities he desired. One was frugality. Quoting adages like "a penny saved is a penny got" and "many mickles make a muckle," he cautioned that "nothing should be bot. that can be made, or done without." A second attribute was diligence: "I expect my people will work from day-breaking until it is dusk in the evening," he wrote from Philadelphia in 1793. On another occasion he voiced his expectation "that my people may . . . be diligent while they are at [their work] . . . lost labour can never be regained — the presumption being, that, every labourer (male or female) does as much in the 24 hours as their strength, without endangering their health, or constitution, will allow of." A third desired attribute was consistent honesty and integrity. "It is established as a maxim in my mind," he asserted, "that, a man who will do wrong to another in one instance, knowingly, will have no scruple in doing it in every instance where it can be done without being liable to discovery." Finally, no personal trait was more important than sobriety: "The inevitable effects of drinking disincline the hands from work[,] hence begins sloth." Although willing to tolerate drunkenness on four days at Christmas time and two each at Easter and Whitsuntide, Washington regularly specified that anyone he employed should be sober most of the time. Thus he dismissed the best miller he had ever had because "his propensity to liquor, & his turbulent temper when under the intoxicating doses of it, were not to be borne." In sum, the ideal Mount Vernon laborer was conscientious, diligent, and self-disciplined or internally controlled. Thus even for his slaves, Washington articulated fundamental elements associated with free labor ideology.[17]

To bring workers to perform their "duty," as he called it, their superiors had to set an example, beginning with himself. Almost every day when he was at home, Washington rode a circuit of some twenty miles and personally inspected the outlying farms. In 1797 he boasted that "I begin my diurnal course with the Sun; . . . if my hirelings are not in their places at that time I send them messages expressive of my sorrow for their indisposition." A visiting Englishman who in 1785 observed this routine subsequently wrote, "He is quite a Cincinnatus, and often works with his men himself; strips off his coat and labors like a common man." When the Marquis de Lafayette arrived unexpectedly at Mount Vernon in 1784, he "found him in the routine of his estate . . . . completely involved with all the details of his lands and house."[18]

Beyond such attentiveness, successful management of labor required "head work," including the ability to conceptualize temporally, so that tasks could be optimally scheduled. Thus on New Year's Day of 1789, Washington issued a detailed plan of work to be accomplished during the coming year — "a full and comprehensive view of my designs." Nothing was to be left to chance.[19]

Immediately below the commander-in-chief of the plantation was the farm manager, or superintendent, whose essential obligation was "to direct the Overseers how to apply the labour to advantage." This demanded both skillful planning and supervision, "For take two Managers and give to each the same number of labourers and let those labourers be equal in all respects. Let both these managers rise equally early — go equally late to rest — be equally active, sober & industrious — and yet in the course of the year one of them, without pushing the hands which are under him more than the other, shall have performed infinitely more work" because of "that fore thought and arrangement which will guard against the mis-application of labour and doing it unseasonably." Displaying his strong sense of social hierarchy, Washington advised the farm manager to maintain "a proper distance" from the overseers, lest familiarity undermine his authority. But the manager was never to be absent from work because "example, be it good or bad, will be followed by all those who look up to you. Keep every one in their places, and to their duty; relaxation from, or neglects in small matters, lead to like attempts in matters of greater magnitude." He especially depended on the resident manager during his protracted absences from home and preferred to fill the position with a trusted relative whenever possible.[20]

The white and black overseers of the individual farms, who came next in the labor hierarchy, were not necessarily required to perform manual labor but were constantly to supervise those who did. Washington informed one recently hired overseer that he "must stir early and late" and that "the only way to keep [people] . . . at work without severity, or wrangling, is always to be with them." Such attentiveness alone would ensure that tasks were accomplished, peace and quiet maintained. Overseers also took responsibility for distributing slave rations and watching over the sick. Davy, a slave overseer for many years, won his master's respect for performing "as well as the white Overseers, and with more quietness than any of them."[21]

Artisans, both white and black, came next in the labor hierarchy. To supplement the skills of his own slaves, and acquire skills that they lacked, Washington engaged the services of white wage earners and a few indentured servants and redemptioners, so that the broad spectrum of 18th-century labor, from slave to free, was represented at Mount Vernon. During the 1780s and 1790s, as he proceeded with

In 1796, Benjamin Latrobe commented that Mount Vernon's "good fences, clear grounds and extensive cultivation" was "uncommon in this part of the world."

his ambitious vision for his estate, he searched as far away as Baltimore, Philadelphia, and even Holland for the joiners, masons, gardeners, weavers, and other artisans he needed. "If they are good workmen, they may be of Assia, Africa, or Europe," he claimed. "They may be Mahometans, Jews, or Christian of any Sect — or they may be Athiests." All were supposed to be "orderly and well disposed people" who "faithfully and industriously perform[ed]" their duties and set an example for one another. Thus, a slave woman named Doll "must be taught to Knit, and *made* to do a sufficient days work of it; otherwise (if suffered to be idle) many more will walk in her Steps."[22]

In written labor agreements, free white artisans were able to negotiate important distances from their enslaved counterparts. They not only collected wages but also received better food allotments as well as washing, mending, and shoe repair. Although the agreements did not specify the same dawn-to-dusk regimen required of slaves, free white workers nonetheless were expected to work hard, report and make up any lost time, and be absent on personal business no more than one day in every three-month period. A house carpenter and joiner named Thomas Green, whose skills were especially needed, successfully bargained for slightly more favorable terms in 1786 when Washington agreed to allow him "not exceeding half a day in a month if his business abroad should indispensably require it . . . but this indulgence is not to be claimed as a perquisite unless real business should actually call him from home." Perhaps because Philip Bater presented himself as a superior gardener, something that Washington valued highly, Bater negotiated an agreement in which he was *paid* to get drunk: "four Dollars at Christmas, with which he may be drunk 4 days and 4 nights; two Dollars at Easter to effect the same purpose; two dollars also at Whitsontide, to be drunk two days." The rest of the year, however, he promised to "conduct himself soberly, diligently and honestly."[23]

Toiling at the bottom of the pyramidal labor hierarchy, enslaved field hands comprised the majority of Mount Vernon's laborers (and a majority of the field hands were female by the 1780s). Even from them the master wanted superior industriousness, and he seems to have assumed that they should take pride in their work and be mindful of "their own reputation." In tending the crops, butchering livestock, digging ditches, filling gullies, cutting timber, building fences, spreading manure, hauling ice uphill from the river to the ice house, and performing ceaseless other tasks, field hands were to "do their duty by fair means" and to accomplish their tasks carefully and "well," even "perfectly." Nor would it do for them ever to be idle and without "sufficient employment."[24]

Ironically, Washington hoped to extract exemplary labor from his slaves without resorting to the most potent incentives any master had: the whip, dividing families, and selling unruly blacks to the West Indies or other dreaded realms. For reasons that are not entirely clear, his attitudes toward slavery and about how his blacks should be treated changed significantly during the years he commanded the army. Certainly he saw the incongruity between his leading the War for Independence while also owning an increasing number of blacks. Surely he recognized the dichotomy between chattel slavery and a revolution justified in terms of natural rights and human liberty. Especially while in Pennsylvania, where the legislature in 1780 became the first in the world to enact gradual emancipation, he could not avoid abolitionist sentiment. And within the army itself, some of the officers he most respected, especially Lafayette, fervently opposed human bondage. Whatever the specific catalysts, Washington developed scruples against selling his blacks at public auction, drew back from separating slave families, and by 1778 muttered about "Negroes (of whom I every day long more and more to get clear of)." Although he occasionally wavered, by the 1780s he resolved not to buy or sell blacks. "I am principled against this kind of traffic in the human species," he declared, and "to disperse the families I have an aversion." Furthermore, he ordered a halt to whipping and advised that discipline usually was better accomplished by "watchfulness and admonition, than by severity." There was not a little irony in Washington's abstaining from proven means of extracting slave labor precisely when the work load at Mount Vernon expanded enormously in order to realize his grand vision of a model plantation.[25]

Washington ordered that all the sheep on his plantation be brought together in a single flock so that they could be watched constantly. But he noted that a slave should not be trusted with the responsibility.

That the laboring hands accomplished much work is evident from the well known 1793 survey map showing the location of the five farms, the numbered fields, and the buildings; in the landscape design, contoured grounds, and structures that survive today; in contemporary paintings and Samuel Vaughan's plan of the Mansion House Farm; in the weekly farm reports and managers' correspondence; and in accounts written by people who visited the estate during the late 18th century. When Benjamin Latrobe approached Mount Vernon in 1796, he found "Good fences, clear grounds and extensive cultivation [that] strike the eye as something uncommon in this part of the World." Samuel Vaughan, after commenting that Washington was "always making experiments," pronounced the five farms "neat, kept perfectly clean & in prime order," while Julian Ursyn Niemcewicz marveled at "vast fields covered with different kinds of grain." Adjacent to the Mansion House, Latrobe described "a neat flower garden laid out in squares, and boxed with great precission," a parterre "trimmed with infinite care," and, on the Potomac River side of the house, densely planted shrubs and trees that "are kept so low as not to interrupt the view but merely to furnish an agreeable border to the extensive prospect beyond." Without acknowledging the work of the manual laborers

A Meteorological Acc.t of the Weather kept at Mt Vernon

August

4th In the morning 70. S.E. Clear 85 S.W. Clear 83 S.W. Clear
5 .... 74 S.W. Clear 86 S.W. Clear 83 S.W. Clear
6 .... 76 S.W. Clear 81 S.W. Clear 79 S.W. Clear
7 .... 73 N.W. Clear 79 S.E. Cloudy 84 S.W. Clear
8 .... 75 S.E. Cloudy 80 S.E. Raining 79 S.E. Raining
9 .... 75 S.W. Cloudy 79 N.W. Clear 76 N.W. Clear
10 .... 70 N.W. Clear 79 S.W. Clear 76 S.W. Clear

August 10th 1793

Dr. Mansion House Farm for the work of of 14 hands An ? ? ? to
10 84 days 84

Cr. By Waggon horses hauling hay with ropes to Stack & ? 2
By Do hauling hay from gravel walk next the lawn, & Clover
from Oat field to Stable loft ? day, & Stopt by rain &c 1
By Do at River Farm 2, Stopt Godfrey with house gang 1 3
By Cart horses hauly hay with ropes to Stack Do 2 in Town 1 3
By hauly lime Sand & Water to the New Barn 1 day & ?, Stopt by rain ? 2
By lime & Sand to Man. House Kitchen, & meal from Mill ? day
and working with house gang ? a day 1
By Single horse cart ? Idle Godfrey Sick 6 days 6
By carrying hay from lawn to gravel Walk, & loading waggon
& Clover in Oat field raking & receiving it in the Stable loft 4
By attending Tom Davis 6, working at Brick yard & new ? ? 11 17
By 6 hands curing grass at Bogue run ? a day Stopt by rain ? ? 6
By mowing the Swamps at Bogue run 3, Landing ? ?
lime kiln 1 4
By pitch'g hay to Stacks at Bogue run 3, & working with yard ? 4
By mellowing the potatoe field after the rain 6, Cook'g ? 8
By Sarah milky churning, & hackling flax 3 3
By Sickness Alley a 2
By Jack in care of Granary & lime kiln 6 Frank in care
of the Cattle 6 Peter in care of the Stables ? 6 18
                                                        84

Rec'd from Mill 23 bush.t of meal. Stock 15 head of Cattle
1 Veal Calf, 4 work Mules, 5 Jacks, 6 Jennys, 4 work horses
2 Saddle Do 1 mare & 1 Stud horse

(they who actually rearranged and maintained the scenery, cleared and tended the fields, cared for the livestock, and built structures as large as the greenhouse-slave-quarter complex and the Dogue Run barn), visitors to the estate easily credited Washington with being "the best . . . farmer in the State." Even more, reported the young Englishman Robert Hunter, "his greatest pride now is to be thought the first farmer in America." This image long outlived Washington.[26]

But what about the workers, black and white, whom the visitors largely ignored? What did *they* think of Washington's incessant planning and prodding, organizing and ordering about? How did they react to his fervent hope that Mount Vernon would inspire the citizenry of the entire nation? We cannot know, for the laboring hands left no written statements to match their master's. His perspective, inevitably incomplete, is the only one that survives. Almost certainly it is also inaccurate to some extent, the view of a man acutely talented at finding fault with others and forcefully expressing his dissatisfactions. But whatever their inadequacies, Washington's words are all that we have.

Where he wanted order and perfection, the laborers seem to have been satisfied with sufficiency and minimal exertion. Consider the post and rail fences on the outlying farms. The rails were so long and thin that they warped and were "unable to bear the weight of a Child in getting over them." Any strong man could "break [them] across his knee." "Is it not to be wondered," Washington complained, "that . . . field No.7 at the River Plantation should want a New Post and Rail fence when it is seen what kind my people make (in spite of all I can do to prevent it)[?]" When he required slaves to redo some fencing, he spoke of "atonement."[27]

By the late 1780s, whether Washington was at home or tending to the affairs of state, his writings reveal a good deal of exasperation. For example: "Every place where I have been there are *many* workmen, and *little* work." Or, regarding the ditchers: "they made a miserable hand of Ditching in Easter week." And a building "so framed as the Dogue run Barn is intended to be ought not to be entrusted to my Negro Carpenters or any other bungler."[28]

The behavior of some men and women particularly provoked his ire. An overseer named James Butler seemingly "has no more authority over the Negroes . . . than an old woman would have; and is as unable to get a proper days Work done by them as she would unless led to it by their own inclination wch. I know is not the case." Of the white carpenter who negotiated up to half a day's absence per month, Washington complained that "Hardly any weekly report comes to hand by which it does not appear that Thos. Greene is absent one or more days. . . . this custom is a bad one, contrary to any ideas I entertained when he was bargained with." So, too, with some of the slaves. When cellar windows needed insulation against winter weather, Washington asserted, "Frank knows how, and should be made to do it . . . otherwise he will be ruined by idleness." As to Isaac, whom Washington blamed for the loss of an entire building, he deserved "a severe punishment for the House, Tools, and seasoned stuff which has been burned by his carelessness." Finally there was Peter, a stableman who seems to have followed his own inclinations: "I have long suspected that [he] . . . under pretence of riding about the Plantations to look after the Mares, Mules, &ca:, is in pursuit of other objects . . . more advancive of his own pleasures than my benefit."[29]

If Washington and his farm managers were correct, slaves also clandestinely extracted a price for the labor they performed by appropriating the master's property for their own use or for sale. In fact, he eventually concluded that anything not nailed down at Mount Vernon was in danger of being stolen. And how could it be nailed down when even the nails were disappearing? "I cannot conceive how it is possible that 6000 twelve penny nails could be used in the Corn house at River Plant[atio]n, but of one thing I have no great doubt and that is, if they can be applied to other uses, or converted into cash, rum, or other things, there will be no scruple in doing it." He required the weekly counting of his livestock partly in an attempt to prevent or at least reduce what he called "atrocious villainies." And he recommended even more frequent tallies of sheep and hogs — "articles most likely to be depredated upon." For, "As the Overseers . . . conduct matters, a Sheep, or a Hog or two, may, every week, be taken without suspicion of it for months. An enquiry then

To keep deer from eating his young fruit trees, Washington used a living fence – a hedge of close-knit shrubs – in combination with a fence and ditch. A similar combination of deterrents is used today at Washington's Fruit Garden & Nursery.

comes too late; and I shall have to submit to one robbery after another, until I shall have nothing left to be robbed of."[30]

As vigorously as he issued work orders, Washington thought of ways to thwart the robberies and instill discipline in the plantation's labor force. The 16-sided barn in which he took such pride would be, in essence, a jail for wheat, complete with iron bars on the windows and heavy locks on the doors. To prevent "embezzlement," seeds were to be mixed with sand and dirt in equal amounts, and broken and worn tools turned in before replacements were issued. Nails were to be rationed, and comparison made between the number issued to carpenters and the number actually hammered into beams and planks. All of the sheep from the five plantations were to be brought together into one flock and watched constantly, but not under the supervision of any slave: "I know not the Negro among all mine, whose capacity, integrity, and attention could be relied on for such a trust as this."[31]

Washington also sought to limit the movement of people and goods onto and off his property. Slaves from other plantations were prohibited from visiting the Mansion House Farm unless their husbands or wives lived there, which was an effort to stop what he called "that spirit of thieving and house breaking, which has got to such a height among my People, or their associates." Overseers were to visit slave quarters at unexpected hours, and lie in wait along the roads to catch anyone making off with goods. The inhabitants of Alexandria, nine miles away, were warned not to buy anything from Mount Vernon slaves unless they carried a certificate "specifying the nature, quality and quantity of the articles" offered for sale. And on and on. The more Washington tried to control his laborers, the less control he seemed to have.[32]

By the last decade of his life, the master and reputable farmer knew that Mount Vernon and its labor force would not, in his lifetime, attain the model of industriousness and productivity with which he so wanted to inspire the young nation. The reasons are complex. From the perspective of the Chesapeake region, independence of the British empire forced wrenching economic adjustments, not least, severe postwar depression, exclusion of American grain and other commodities from the British West Indies, and collapse of trade with much of Europe after the Continent plunged into the Napoleonic wars. Although no longer a typical Chesapeake planter, Washington could not escape the economic difficulties that long plagued the region. Nor did he live to see any but the most rudimentary realization of his dreams for a national capital on the banks of the Potomac, or river and canal access to the interior of the continent.[33]

At Mount Vernon itself, agricultural experimentation necessarily entailed substantial risks. No one could know in advance whether English cultivation practices, Russian wheat, homemade plows, and all the other innovations would actually produce the dramatic, and economically viable, transformation that Washington envisioned. He never lost his enthusiasm for agricultural reform, but the plantation proved to be a severe trial. Adversity thwarted him again and again. Seeds shipped from other states failed to arrive in time for planting, thereby delaying experimentation for a year and "deranging" carefully contrived schedules for crop rotation. Drought ruined crops, rains opened gullies, winds blew down the hedges, insects invaded the fields, and even an attempt to renew a field with silt dredged from the Potomac River bottom ended in disaster. Laced with naturally occurring toxic chemicals washed down from the Appalachian Mountains, the silt poisoned the land for more than a hundred years.[34]

In the end, ironically, and for all his passion to improve his lands, the reputable farmer's methods substantially damaged them. Traditional tobacco cultivation was characterized by rather casual clearing of the land, sequential planting of tobacco and grain for several years, then letting the land lie fallow until fertility returned. Cultivation rotated from field to field. With the mixed-grain agriculture introduced at Mount Vernon, fields were cultivated continuously and replenished through fertilizers and rotation of crops. Farm machinery, which replaced the ax and hoe, required fields free of potentially damaging obstructions such as tree roots and stumps, and such machinery tilled the soil much more deeply. In making the transition from tobacco to grain, Washington firmly believed that he was abandoning destructive practices, in favor of new methods that would both enhance productivity and improve the ecology of his land. He, and other Chesapeake farmers who made the

This report from Washington's lead carpenter reflects how many hours were required for each slave to accomplish a specific task.

same transition during the late 18th century, did not adequately appreciate that long-fallow cultivation, if properly practiced, was ecologically sound, whereas the new mode of agriculture would lead to massive erosion and soil degradation.[35]

Another major problem, from his perspective, was the increasing size of the slave population. Washington's disinclination to sell off slaves — in essence his refusal to apply to the plantation's demographics the same rationalizing impulse directed at its land and crops — led to a population explosion (which almost certainly contributed to the fervency with which he created work assignments). Between 1786, when he already felt "over stocked" with blacks, and 1799, the year of his death, the number of African Americans at the Potomac farms jumped from 216 to 317. During the summer of 1799 Washington lamented that "on this Estate (Mount Vernon) I have more working Negros by a full moiety, than can be employed to any advantage in the farming system, and I shall never turn Planter thereon. To sell the overplus I cannot, because I am principled against this kind of traffic in the human species. To hire them out, is almost as bad, because they could not be disposed of in families to any advantage, and to disperse the families I have an aversion. What then is to be done? Something must or I shall be ruined . . . ."[36]

Among all the problems, however, none were more compelling and poignant than those of the African-American slaves. The idealism of the Revolutionary generation sometimes knew no bounds, and the Revolution itself made many people contemplate the glaring inequity of chattel slavery thriving in a nation founded upon principles of human liberty. The mature Washington would not have argued that slavery was a necessary evil, much less a positive good. Although he had no sympathy for the activities of abolitionist groups and probably was embarrassed when Pennsylvanians named an antislavery society after him, he nevertheless hoped that state legislatures eventually would enact gradual emancipation, and he spoke of personally laying "a foundation to prepare the rising generation for a destiny different from that in which they were born." Yet, in words that Abraham Lincoln would echo as late as the Civil War, Washington hoped that emancipation would proceed *so* gradually that slavery would disappear by "imperceptable degrees."[37]

On balance, Washington felt profoundly ambivalent about the slave system and about blacks in America, in no small part because of his experiences as a slave owner. Far from the rarefied debates in the Constitutional Convention and early Congresses, his attitudes about African Americans were shaped and constantly honed at Mount Vernon. It seems never to have occurred to him that a crucial element was missing in his grand design for the estate. Namely, his cause was not the cause of the laboring hands. Where slaves were unwilling to internalize his work ethic, he adjudged them ignorant and lazy. If they took no pride in their work, he was sure they were slovenly. And where we can see the cleverness with which slaves made his property their own (assuming they did), Washington saw only deceit. Rational mechanisms blacks adopted to cope with their condition and the demands placed upon them led their master to conclude that they were lazy and untrustworthy — just the opposite of the industrious, conscientious citizenry upon whom the very survival of the republic was thought to depend. This attitude, which countless whites shared, was virtually a precondition for Justice Roger B. Taney's opinion, in the Dred Scott case, denying black people citizenship.[38]

Washington was the most influential man in Revolutionary America, living in the state that had over 40 percent of the slave population of the United States, according to the 1790 Federal census. No one was better positioned to speak out against the continuing enslavement of half a million African Americans. But while he privately anguished over slavery, he remained publicly silent about it. Although he periodically considered seating newly freed blacks as tenant farmers, something Lafayette urged him to undertake, nothing came of the idea. Nor, during his final years — years during which northern states adopted gradual emancipation, thousands of Chesapeake masters privately manumitted slaves, and the first substantial free black populations developed in the United States — did Washington respond to entreaties that he, among all Americans, should set an example by promptly liberating his own chattel and endorsing general abolition.[39]

In 1799, when he wrote the most famous manumission in American history into his will, it was not a joyful act. Washington freed his slaves because he did not know what else to do with Mount Vernon's burgeoning black population. He had little faith, moreover, that African Americans would do well and fare well in the young republic. But Mount Vernon slaves, displaying an optimism born of the Revolution, wanted the chance to try. In 1797 they confided to a party of visiting Frenchmen that "they hoped they would no longer be slaves in ten years." They had a powerful vision of their own.[40]

NOTES

The author gratefully acknowledges financial support from the Carter G. Woodson Institute for Afro-American and African Studies at the University of Virginia and the Graduate School of the University of Wisconsin-Madison. Generous encouragement and suggestions came from Rhys Isaac, Christopher F. Lee, the late Armstead Robinson, Philip J. Schwarz, Lucia C. Stanton, and the staffs of the Mount Vernon Ladies' Association of the Union (especially Ellen M. Clark, Barbara McMillan, Christine Meadows, Dennis J. Pogue, John Riley, and Mary V. Thompson) and the *Papers of George Washington* editorial project (especially W. W. Abbot, Philander D. Chase, and Dorothy Twohig). Sarah Costello, Charlotte Haller, and Deborah Buchman Stubbs provided valuable research assistance. Fuller development of the interpretation advanced in this essay will appear in the author's *Mount Vernon and the Nation: From the Revolution to the Civil War* (New York, forthcoming).

1. Rhys Isaac, "The Enlightenment and the Problems of Systematizing the Plantation: Colonel Landon Carter's Sabine Hall, 1756-1778," paper presented at a conference on "Re-creating the World of the Virginia Plantation, 1750-1820" (Charlottesville, Va., 1990); idem, "Identities in an 18th-Century Enlightenment Diary: Colonel Landon Carter's Conflicted Virginia Plantation World, 1756-1778" (unpublished paper, 1991); Jack P. Greene, ed., The Diary of Colonel Landon Carter of Sabine Hall, 1752-1778, 2 vols. (Charlottesville, Va., 1965), 1:403.

2. Richard S. Dunn, "Annual Work Rhythms on Mount Airy," paper presented at a conference on "Re-creating the World of the Virginia Plantation, 1750-1820." On English agriculture, see G. E. Fussell, "Science and Practice in Eighteenth-Century British Agriculture," *Agricultural History* 43 (1969), 7-18; Roy Porter, *English Society in the Eighteenth Century* (London, 1982), 221-22; Ian R. Christie, *Wars and Revolutions: Britain, 1760-1815* (London, 1982), 4-6.

3. Edwin M. Betts, ed., *Thomas Jefferson's Farm Book: With Commentary and Relevant*

Extracts from Other Writings (Princeton, N. J., 1953), especially 50-53, 426-53; idem, ed., *Thomas Jefferson's Garden Book, 1766-1824: With Relevant Extracts from His Other Writings* (Philadelphia, 1944); Duc de La Rochefoucauld-Liancourt, "A Frenchman Views Jefferson the Farmer," in Visitors to Monticello, ed. Merrill D. Peterson (Charlottesville, Va., 1989), 25-28; Dumas Malone, *Jefferson and His Times*, 6 vols. (Boston, 1948-81), vol. 3: *Jefferson and the Ordeal of Liberty*, 194.

4. Bruce A. Ragsdale, "George Washington, the British Tobacco Trade, and Economic Opportunity in Prerevolutionary Virginia," *Virginia Magazine of History and Biography* 97 (1989), 133-45.

5. Dennis J. Pogue, *Archaeology at George Washington's Mount Vernon, 1931-1987* (Mount Vernon, Va., 1988); idem, "Mount Vernon: Transformation of an Eighteenth-Century Plantation System," in *Historical Archaeology of the Chesapeake*, ed. Paul A. Shackel and Barbara J. Little (Washington, D. C., 1994), 101-14; Elizabeth K. de Forest, *The Gardens and Grounds at Mount Vernon: How George Washington Planned and Planted Them* (Mount Vernon, Va., 1982), which reproduces Samuel Vaughan's plan on p. xii; Julian Ursyn Niemcewicz, *Under Their Vine and Fig Tree: Travels through America in 1797-1799, 1805 . . .* , trans. and ed. Metchie J. E. Budka (Elizabeth, N. J., 1965), 98. Contemporary sources with rather full descriptions of Mount Vernon include, in addition to Niemcewicz, Louis B. Wright and Marion Tinling, eds., *Quebec to Carolina in 1785-1786: Being the Travel Diary and Observations of Robert Hunter, Jr., a Young Merchant of London* (San Marino, Calif., 1943), 191-98; the Journal of Samuel Powel, 1787 (Historical Society of Pennsylvania, Philadelphia), fols. 2-6; J. P. Brissot de Warville, *New Travels in the United States of America, 1788*, ed. Durand Echeverria (Cambridge, Mass., 1964), 342-43; and Edward C. Carter II et al., eds., *The Virginia Journals of Benjamin Henry Latrobe, 1795-1798*, 2 vols. (New Haven, Conn., 1977), 1:161-73. For a nuanced treatment of the cultural meaning and significance of plantation architecture, consult Rhys Isaac, *The Transformation of Virginia, 1740-1790* (Chapel Hill, N. C., 1982), chap. 2. See also Camille Wells, "The Eighteenth-Century Landscape of Virginia's Northern Neck," *Northern Neck of Virginia Historical Magazine* 37 (1987), 423-46, and Mechal Sobel, *The World They Made Together: Black and White Values in Eighteenth-Century Virginia* (Princeton, N. J., 1987), chap. 10.

6. Mount Vernon book list, July 23, 1783, George Washington Papers (Manuscript Division, Library of Congress), microfilm reel 92; Ragsdale, "George Washington, the British Tobacco Trade, and Economic Opportunity in Prerevolutionary Virginia," 145-61; Douglas Southall Freeman et al., *George Washington: A Biography*, 7 vols. (New York, 1948-57), 3:295-96. Niemcewicz, *Under Their Vine and Fig Tree*, 100-103. Washington told David Humphreys, his biographer, that before the war he raised approximately seven thousand bushels of wheat and ten thousand of corn annually. Rosemarie Zagarri, ed., *David Humphreys' "Life of General Washington," with George Washington's "Remarks"* (Athens, Ga., 1991), 24. In his area of the Chesapeake during the colonial period, Washington was unusual in the extent to which he forsook tobacco

production, not because he diversified his operations. Cf. Lois Green Carr and Lorena S. Walsh, "Economic Diversification and Labor Organization in the Chesapeake, 1650-1820," in *Work and Labor in Early America*, ed. Stephen Innes (Chapel Hill, N. C., 1988), 144-84. For transition to grain cultivation on the Atlantic coastal plain, consult Paul G. E. Clemens, *The Atlantic Economy and Colonial Maryland's Eastern Shore: From Tobacco to Grain* (Ithaca, N. Y., 1980). A macroeconomic interpretation of this process, emphasizing accelerated change during the last quarter of the 18th century, is Carville Earle, "The Myth of the Southern Soil Miner: Macrohistory, Agricultural Innovation, and Environmental Change," in *The Ends of the Earth: Perspectives on Modern Environmental History*, ed. Donald Worster (New York, 1988), 175-210. See also David Klingaman, "The Significance of Grain in the Development of the Tobacco Colonies," *Journal of Economic History* 29 (1969), 268-78, and Harold B. Gill, Jr., "Wheat Culture in Colonial Virginia," *Agricultural History* 52 (1978), 380-93.

7. Information on Washington's acquisition of African Americans through marriage and inheritance is contained in W. W. Abbot et al., eds., *The Papers of George Washington*, 48 vols. to date (Charlottesville, Va., 1976 -), Colonial Series, 1:227-31 and 6:217-19, 311-13. Slave purchases are mentioned in ibid., 1:313, 4:96-98, 8:244-45, 9:57, 222. Growth of the slave population may be traced in annual lists of taxables, as, for example, those for 1771-73 in ibid., 8:479-80, 9:54-55, 238-39. The term "species of property" appears in Washington to John Francis Mercer, Dec. 5, 1786, *Papers: Confederation Ser.*, 4:442. For examples of discipline, see Papers: Colonial Ser., 5:447, 7:453-54.

8. Madison to William Eustis, July 6, 1819, quoted in Drew R. McCoy, *The Last of the Fathers: James Madison and the Republican Legacy* (New York, 1989), 73, and also 262; circular letter to the states, June 8, 1783, and Washington to Dr. James Anderson, Apr. 25, 1793, in *The Writings of George Washington from the Original Manuscript Sources, 1745-1799*, ed. John C. Fitzpatrick, 39 vols. (Washington, D. C., 1931-44), 26:485, 32:432; Journal of Samuel Powel, 1787, fol. 4. Americans' perceptions of the transcendent importance of the Revolution are conveyed in Gordon S. Wood, *The Creation of the American Republic, 1776-1787* (Chapel Hill, N. C., 1969), 46-48, 118-22, Henry F. May, *The Enlightenment in America* (New York, 1976), 161-64, and Merrill D. Peterson, *Adams and Jefferson: A Revolutionary Dialogue* (Athens, Ga., 1976), chap. 1.

9. Washington to Robert Morris, Feb. 1, 1785, James Madison, Nov. 17, 1788, Moustier, Dec. 15, 1788, William Pearce, Dec. 18, 1793, and Sir John Sinclair, Dec. 11, 1796, *Papers: Confederation Ser.*, 2:309-15, Papers: Presidential Ser., 1:112-14, 181, *Writings*, 33:195, 35:328-29; Journal of Samuel Powel, fol. 5; Louis-Philippe, *Diary of My Travels in America: Louis-Philippe, King of France, 1830-1848*, trans. Stephen Becker (New York, 1977), 24; Douglas R. Littlefield, "Eighteenth-Century Plans to Clear the Potomac River: Technology, Expertise, and Labor in a Developing Nation," *Virginia Magazine of History and Biography* 93 (1985), 291-93, 305-06; Wilbur E. Garrett, "George Washington's

Patowmack Canal: Waterway That Led to the Constitution," *National Geographic* 171 (1987), 716-53; Stanley Elkins and Eric McKitrick, *The Age of Federalism* (New York, 1993), 169-70; Merritt Roe Smith, *Harpers Ferry Armory and the New Technology: The Challenge of Change* (Ithaca, N. Y., 1977), 27-33; Fort Washington, Maryland (Washington, D. C., n.d.); David L. Salay, "'very picturesque, but regarded as nearly useless': Fort Washington, Maryland, 1816-1872," *Maryland Historical Magazine* 81 (1986), 67-69.

10. Wright and Tinling, eds., *Quebec to Carolina in 1785-1786: Being the Travel Diary and Observations of Robert Hunter, Jr.*, 195; slave census, Feb. 18, 1786, in Donald Jackson and Dorothy Twohig, eds., *The Diaries of George Washington*, 6 vols. (Charlottesville, Va., 1976-79), 4:277-83; slave census, ca. June 1799, *Writings*, 37:268. The most sensitive treatment of slave life at Mount Vernon is Mary V. Thompson, "And Procure for Themselves a Few Amenities: The Private Life of George Washington's Slaves," *Virginia Cavalcade* 48 (1999), 178-90.

11. The quotations are in Washington to the Marquis de Lafayette, Feb. 1, 1784, George William Fairfax, June 30, 1785, Arthur Young, Aug. 6, 1786, and Nov. 1, 1787, and David Stuart, Feb. 7, 1796, *Papers: Confederation Ser.*, 1:87-88, 3:89, 4:196-97, *Writings*, 29:296-300, 34:453; Moustier to Washington, Nov. 26, 1788, *Papers: Presidential Ser.*, 1:127. For farming plans mentioned in the text, see *Papers: Confederation Ser.*, 4:13, 197, 371-72, 484-85, *Writings*, 29:215, 231, 282, 388, 456, 32:237, 277, and *Papers: Presidential Ser.*, 1:91-93, 160-62. Arthur Young's influence on agriculture in the United States is assessed in Rodney C. Loehr, "Arthur Young and American Agriculture," *Agricultural History* 43 (1969), 46-56.

12. Washington to Thomas Jefferson, Jan. 1, 1788, Charles Carter, Jan. 20, 1788, Samuel Chamberline, Apr. 3, 1788, and Anthony Whiting, Aug. 14, 1792, *Writings*, 29:351, 388, 455, 32:180; Moustier to Washington, Nov. 26, 1788, *Papers: Presidential Ser.*, 1:127. In his last message to Congress, on December 7, 1796, Washington asserted that, "It will not be doubted, that with reference either to individual, or National Welfare, Agriculture is of primary importance." Writings, 35:315. He clearly was as convinced of the vital significance of agriculture as were the Jeffersonian Republicans. Cf. Drew R. McCoy, *The Elusive Republic: Political Economy in Jeffersonian America* (Chapel Hill, N. C., 1980), 83-85, and Joyce O. Appleby, *Capitalism and a New Social Order: The Republican Vision of the 1790s* (New York, 1984), 87-89.

13. Washington to Carter, Dec. 14, 1787, and Whiting, Oct. 14 and Nov. 18, 1792, *Writings*, 29:336-39, 32:180-81, 228. A list of tasks performed at Mount Vernon in 1786-87, which is organized according to the season of the year and the gender of workers, is in Carr and Walsh, "Economic Diversification and Labor Organization in the Chesapeake, 1650-1820," 185-88.

14. Washington to Whiting, Nov. 18 and 25, Dec. 2, 1792, *Writings*, 32:229, 239, 249. In 1796 Washington recalled that "I transplanted thousands of Pine and Cedar without getting scarcely one to live until I adopted . . . [the frozen] method; after which, so long as it was practised, I never lost one." Washington

to Pearce, May 22, 1796, ibid., 35:67.

15. *Diaries*, 4:271; building instructions for Dogue Run barn [1792], Washington to Whiting, Nov. 11, 1792, Feb. 24, 1793, William Augustine Washington, Mar. 3, 1793, and Pearce, Nov. 2, 1794, Nov. 14, 1796, *Writings*, 32:285-90, 215, 357, 369, 34:15, 35:279, respectively. The repositioned slave dwellings at Union Farm are indicated on Washington's 1793 survey map of the five farms (Huntington Library, San Marino, Calif.), which is reproduced in *Mount Vernon: A Handbook* (Mount Vernon, Va., 1985), 18-19. Dennis J. Pogue describes the novel sixteen-sided barn in "Every Thing Trim, Handsome, and Thriving: Re-creating George Washington's Visionary Farm," *Virginia Cavalcade* 48 (1999), 160-61.

16. Washington to Whiting, Dec. 2, 1792, *Writings*, 32:246; Kenneth R. Bowling and Helen E. Veit, eds., *The Diary of William Maclay and Other Notes on Senate Debates* (Baltimore, 1988), 258. For a general description of the farm reports and the prototype prepared by Washington, Feb. 26, 1785-Apr. 16, 1786, see *Papers: Confederation Ser.*, 3:389-410. Many of the farm managers' reports are in the George Washington Papers at the Library of Congress, the Lloyd W. Smith Collection at Morristown National Historical Park, Morristown, N. J., and the Mount Vernon Ladies' Association of the Union, Mount Vernon, Va. Slave occupations are listed in the 1786 and 1799 censuses, in *Diaries* 4:277-83, and *Writings*, 37:268.

17. Frugality: Washington to Whiting, Dec. 16, 1792, Apr. 21, 1793, *Writings*, 32:262, 423. Diligence: Washington to John Fairfax, Jan. 1, 1789, and Whiting, Jan. 6, 1793, *Papers: Presidential Ser.*, 1:223, *Writings*, 32:293. Honesty: Washington to Whiting, Feb. 10, 1793, *Writings*, 32:338-39. Sobriety: Washington to Robert Lewis & Sons, Feb. 1, 1785, May 18, 1786, and Thomas Green, Mar. 31, 1789, and articles of agreement with Philip Bater, Apr. 23, 1787, *Papers: Confederation Ser.*, 2:317, 4:57, *Papers: Presidential Ser.*, 1:468-69, and *Writings*, 29:206-07. Regarding expectations of slaves, consult, for comparative purposes, Lucia C. Stanton, "'Those Who Labor for My Happiness': Thomas Jefferson and His Slaves," in *Jeffersonian Legacies*, ed. Peter S. Onuf (Charlottesville, Va., 1993), 154-55, and Drew Gilpin Faust, *James Henry Hammond and the Old South: A Design for Mastery* (Baton Rouge, La., 1982), chap. 5. In *The Problem of Slavery in the Age of Revolution, 1770-1823* (Ithaca, N. Y., 1975), 49, 305-06, 358, 455-66, David B. Davis insightfully juxtaposes the coercive external controls typical of slave labor systems with the internal personal discipline that capitalistic employers advocated for their workers.

18. Washington to Whiting, Dec. 23, 1792, and James McHenry, May 29, 1797, *Writings*, 32:275, 35:455; Wright and Tinling, eds., *Quebec to Carolina in 1785-1786: Being the Travel Diary and Observations of Robert Hunter, Jr.*, 195; the Marquis de Lafayette to Adrienne de Noailles de Lafayette, Aug. 20, 1784, in Stanley J. Idzerda et al., eds., *Lafayette in the Age of the American Revolution: Selected Letters and Papers, 1776-1790*, 5 vols. to date (Ithaca, N. Y., 1977-), 5:237. Daily farming activities are recorded in the Diaries.

19. Washington to James Bloxham, Jan. 1, 1789, and J. Fairfax, Jan. 1 and Mar. 31, 1789, *Papers: Presidential Ser.*, 1:208-13, 216-24, 466.

20. Articles of agreement with Bloxham, May 31, 1786, *Papers: Confederation Ser.*, 4:86-88; Washington to George Augustine Washington, June 3, 1787, J. Fairfax, Jan. 1, 1789, Whiting, Oct. 14, 1792, and Pearce, Dec. 18, 1793, *Writings*, 29:226, *Papers: Presidential Ser.*, 1:223-24, *Writings*, 32:184, 33:191, respectively.

21. Articles of agreement with William Garner, Dec. 10, 1788, *Papers: Presidential Ser.*, 1:171-72; Washington to Whiting, Jan. 6, 1793, and Pearce, Dec. 18, 1793, *Writings*, 32:292-93, 33:194.

22. Washington to Tench Tilghman, Mar. 24, 1784, and Philip Marsteller, Nov. 27 and Dec. 15, 1786, *Papers: Confederation Ser.*, 1:232, 4:402-03, 455; articles of agreement with Bater, Apr. 23, 1787, Washington to Nathaniel Ingraham, Mar. 22, 1788, Whiting, Nov. 4, 1792, and Clement Biddle, Nov. 24, 1799, *Writings*, 29:206, 444-45, 32:205, 37:438.

23. Articles of agreement with Thomas Mahony, Aug. 1, 1786, Apr. 15, 1788, Thomas Green, Dec. 6, 1786, and Bater, Apr. 23, 1787, *Papers: Confederation Ser.*, 4:182-83, George Washington Papers, reels 97 and 96, respectively, *Writings*, 29:206-07.

24. Slave census, Feb. 18, 1786, *Diaries*, 4:277-83; Washington to J. Fairfax, Jan. 1, 1789, *Papers: Presidential Ser.*, 1:217; to G. A. Washington, July 1, 1787, and Whiting, Dec. 23, 1792, and Jan. 20, 1793, and slave census, ca. June 1799, *Writings*, 29:240-41, 32:277, 307, 37:268.

25. Arthur Zilversmit, *The First Emancipation: The Abolition of Slavery in the North* (Chicago, 1967), 126-31; Madison to Jefferson, Oct. 17, 1784, in *The Republic of Letters: The Correspondence Between Thomas Jefferson and James Madison, 1776-1826*, ed. James Morton Smith, 3 vols. (New York, 1995), 1:348; Lund Washington to G. Washington, Apr. 8, 1778 (Mount Vernon Ladies' Association of the Union); G. Washington to L. Washington, Aug. 15, 1778, and Feb. 24-26, 1779, John Francis Mercer, Sept. 9 and Nov. 6, 1786, Whiting, May 5, 1793, and Robert Lewis, Aug. 18, 1799, *Writings*, 12:327, 14:148, Papers: Confederation Ser., 4:243, 336; *Writings*, 32:443, 37:338, respectively. After whipping a slave named Charlotte in 1793, on the grounds of impudence, Whiting rather nervously explained that "she threatens me very much with informing Lady Washington when She comes home & says she has not been whipd for 14 Years past." (Washington, from Philadelphia, offered approval to his farm manager.) In 1797 Louis-Philippe reported that "General Washington has forbidden the use of the whip on his blacks." Whiting to Washington, Jan. 16, 1793 (Mount Vernon Ladies' Association of the Union); Washington to Whiting, Jan. 20, 1793, *Writings*, 32:307; Louis-Philippe, *Diary of My Travels in America*, 31-32.

26. Carter et al., eds., *The Virginia Journals of Benjamin Henry Latrobe, 1795-1798*, 1:162-63, 165; Journal of Samuel Vaughan, 1787, fol. 56, Mount Vernon Ladies' Association of the Union; Niemcewicz, *Under Their Vine and Fig Tree*, 100; Wright and Tinling, eds., *Quebec to Carolina, 1785-1786: Being the Travel Diary and Observations of Robert Hunter, Jr.*, 195; Joan E. Cashin, "Landscape and

Memory in Antebellum Virginia," *Virginia Magazine of History and Biography*, 102 (1994), 484-86.

27. Washington to Whiting, Oct. 28, 1792, and June 2, 1793, *Writings*, 32:195-96, 482.

28. Washington to G. A. Washington, June 10 and July 1, 1787, and Whiting, Mar. 3, 1793, ibid., 29:233, 241, 32:365.

29. Washington to G. A. Washington, Sept. 2, 1787, Whiting, Dec. 9, 16, and 30, 1792, and Pearce, Dec. 18, 1793, ibid., 29:269, 32:256, 263, 279, 33:193.

30. Washington to Whiting, Nov. 18 and 25, 1792, and Feb. 3, 1793, ibid., 32:232, 240, 330.

31. Washington to Whiting, Dec. 9, 1792, and Feb. 24, Apr. 21 and 28, May 5 and 19, 1793, ibid., 32:257, 357, 425, 435-36, 442-44, 462-63.

32. Washington to Whiting, Dec. 2, 1792, and May 19, 1793, ibid., 32:246, 465; *Columbian Mirror and Alexandria Gazette* (Alexandria, Va.), June 12, 1798. The author thanks Michael L. Nicholls for calling this advertisement to her attention.

33. On massive economic challenges accompanying the Revolution, see John J. McCusker and Russell R. Menard, *The Economy of British America, 1607-1789* (Chapel Hill, N. C., 1985), chap. 17; Richard B. Morris, *The Forging of the Union, 1781-1789* (New York, 1987), chap. 6 ; and, for an area across the Potomac River from Mount Vernon, Jean B. Lee, *The Price of Nationhood: The American Revolution in Charles County* (New York, 1994), chap. 8. Virginians' efforts to understand and adjust to post-Independence economic change are analyzed in Bruce A. Ragsdale, *A Planters' Republic: The Search for Economic Independence in Revolutionary Virginia* (Madison, Wisc., 1996), chap. 8. Difficulties in building the national capital and developing the Potomac River route to the interior are discussed in Elkins and McKitrick, *The Age of Federalism*, 171-82, and Littlefield, "Eighteenth-Century Plans to Clear the Potomac River," 293-96, 306-09.

34. Washington to Young, Aug. 6, 1786, Mary Washington, Feb. 15, 1787, C. Carter, Dec. 14, 1787, Edward Newenham, Mar. 2, 1789, Embree & Shotwell, Mar. 15, 1789, Whiting, Nov. 25, 1792, and Pearce, Apr. 10, 1796, *Papers: Confederation Ser.*, 4:196, *Writings*, 29:158-59, 336, *Papers: Presidential Ser.*, 1:355, 396-97, *Writings*, 32:238, 35:20, respectively; Carter et al., eds., *The Virginia Journals of Benjamin Henry Latrobe, 1795-1798*, 1:170; Journal of Samuel Powel, 1787, fol. 5. The author wishes to thank David O. Percy for information on Potomac River silt applied to the soil at Mount Vernon.

35. Earle, "The Myth of the Southern Soil Miner," 194-99; Edward C. Papenfuse, "Planter Behavior and Economic Opportunity in a Staple Economy," *Agricultural History* 46 (1972), 297-311; Henry M. Miller, "Transforming a 'Splendid and Delightsome Land': Colonists and Ecological Change in the Chesapeake, 1607-1820," *Journal of the Washington Academy of Sciences* 76 (1986), 182-83; David O. Percy, "Ax or Plow?: Significant Colonial Landscape Alteration Rates in the Maryland and Virginia Tidewater," *Agricultural History* 66 (1992), 66-74.

36. Slave census, Feb. 18, 1786, *Diaries*, 4:277-83; Washington to Mercer, Dec. 19, 1786, and Robert Lewis, Aug. 18, 1799, and slave census, ca. June 1799,

Writings, 29:117, 37:338-39, 268, respectively. Of the African Americans on the 1799 list, Washington owned 124 outright, had a life estate in 153 dower slaves, and had hired another 40.

37. Washington to Morris, Apr. 12, 1786, Lafayette, May 10, 1786, and Mercer, Sept. 9, 1786, *Papers: Confederation Ser.*, 4:15-16, 43-44, 4:243; Zagarri, ed., *David Humphreys' "Life of Washington"*, 78; Richard N. Current, *The Lincoln Nobody Knows* (New York, 1958), 220. Washington's attitudes toward slavery are treated in Dorothy Twohig, "'That Species of Property': Washington's Role in the Controversy Over Slavery," in *George Washington Reconsidered*, ed. Don Higginbotham (Charlottesville, VA., 2001), 114-38. The antislavery society was named "The Washington Society for the Relief of Free Negroes, and Others, Unlawfully Held in Bondage." See *Memorials Presented to the Congress of the United States of America, by the Different Societies Instituted for Promoting the Abolition of Slavery, &c. &c. in the States of Rhode-Island, Connecticut, New-York, Pennsylvania, Maryland, and Virginia* (Philadelphia, 1792), 21. Davis, *The Problem of Slavery in the Age of Revolution, 1770-1823*, remains the most perceptive and nuanced treatment of tensions over slavery during the era of the American Revolution. See also Ira Berlin, *Many Thousands Gone: The First Two Centuries of Slavery in North America* (Cambridge, Mass., 1998); idem and Ronald Hoffman, eds., *Slavery and Freedom in the Age of the American Revolution* (Charlottesville, Va., 1983); Robert W. Fogel, *Without Consent or Contract: The Rise and Fall of American Slavery* (New York, 1989), 240-51; Donald R. Wright, *African Americans in the Colonial Era: From African Origins through the American Revolution* (Arlington Heights, Ill., 1990), chap. 4; idem, *African Americans in the Early Republic, 1789-1831* (Arlington Heights, Ill., 1993); and Peter Kolchin, *American Slavery, 1619-1877* (New York, 1993), chap. 3.

38. Don E. Fehrenbacher, *The Dred Scott Case: Its Significance in American Law and Politics* (New York, 1978), chaps. 14-15.

39. U. S. Census Office, 1st Census, 1790, *Return of the Whole Number of Persons within the Several Districts of the United States, According to "An Act Providing for the Enumeration of the Inhabitants of the United States," Passed March the First, One Thousand Seven Hundred and Ninety-One* (Philadelphia, 1791), 3; Lafayette to Washington, Feb. 5, 1783, in Idzerda et al., eds., *Lafayette in the Age of the American Revolution*, 5:91-92; Robert Pleasants to Washington, Dec. 11, 1785, *Papers: Confederation Ser.*, 3:449-51; Washington to Lafayette, Apr. 5, 1783, and May 10, 1786, *Writings*, 26:300, *Papers: Confederation Ser.*, 4:43-44; Edward Rushton, *Expostulatory Letter to George Washington, of Mount Vernon, in Virginia, on his Continuing to be a Proprietor of Slaves* (Liverpool, 1797); Twohig, "'That Species of Property': Washington's Role in the Controversy over Slavery," 121-23.

40. Washington's manumission and provision for his slaves (he had no control over the disposition of the dower slaves) is in his will, July 9, 1799, *Writings*, 37:276-77. Louis-Philippe recounted the conversation with Mount Vernon slaves in *Diary of My Travels in America*, 32.

Washington depended upon slave labor to accomplish virtually all of the goals he established for expanding the 2000-acre estate he inherited into an 8,000-acre plantation with several "profit centers."

Slavery And Agriculture At Mount Vernon

Lorena S. Walsh

This essay offers a preliminary exploration of the history of slavery and agriculture at Mount Vernon. It approaches the topic largely from the perspective of George Washington and of other contemporary planters and slave owners. The experiences of the enslaved Africans and African Virginians who lived and worked on the Mount Vernon estate in the second half of the 18th century were profoundly shaped by the career and aspirations of their owner. Washington's early penchant for estate building and his evolving agricultural aspirations are a central part of the story of African-Virginian farming at Mount Vernon, as are the inter-meshing seasonal requirements of the various crop mixes that Washington employed.

Equally central are the life experiences and human resources of the enslaved residents of Mount Vernon. These men, women, and children employed the knowledge and skills they possessed to further the productive goals of the estate, to maintain their families and improve their living conditions, and to resist the strenuous demands that Washington tried to impose. So far little is known about who these people were, where they came from, and how their differing prior experiences in Africa and elsewhere in Virginia contributed to the ways they organized their private lives and interacted with their owner, supervisors, and others living on and around Mount Vernon.

Early in his career, Washington's primary aim was to build a large estate and become a rich man. At the end of the Revolution he had first to make up for income lost during the war and to rebuild a badly neglected farm. By 1785 his aims had become more ambitious — to make Mount Vernon a model of improved agriculture that other Americans might emulate. Since this work was undertaken almost entirely by the slaves, new systems of slave management were as crucial to the success of Washington's plans as were new systems of farm management and new agricultural techniques. The sheer scale and geographic concentration of his operation required innovative labor management strategies. Washington ranked among the top two dozen largest slave holders in the Chesapeake in the 1780s and 90s, and probably was one of no more than half a dozen who concentrated so much labor on so few acres.[1]

Washington's aspirations led him to expect more from his enslaved workers than did less ambitious and less self-disciplined planters. During the times when he was in residence, Washington subjected Mount Vernon laborers to exacting daily personal supervision and intensified work requirements. As Jean Lee argues in an essay in this volume, Washington wanted these men and women to develop levels of industry and internal self discipline that matched the exacting standards he demanded of himself.

Climate and the seasonal requirements of the major field crops also shaped the outer contours of the slaves' lives — dictating periods of intense effort and periods of greater ease, demanding lesser or greater inputs of judgment and skill, and impacting on daily work conditions and on the way work was organized. Consequently the

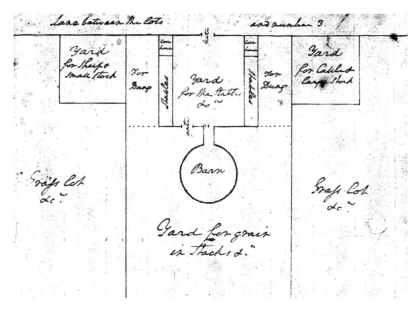

This architectural sketch in Washington's hand outlines the design for his new treading barn, stables, and storage structures, which have now been reconstructed on the Mount Vernon estate.

first task is to trace Washington's changing decisions about crop mix, and the effects of these decisions for the workers.

In the 1750s slaves at Mount Vernon raised the traditional Chesapeake triad of tobacco, corn, and wheat, crops which all but a few newly-arrived Africans had been tending for decades on farms scattered across the colony, and some, for three or more generations in Virginia. Over the years Washington dropped or curtailed two of the three traditional staples — tobacco and corn — and added an almost unprecedented array of new crops and improved livestock. From the mid 1780s laborers had to undertake risky projects that involved much learning by trial and error. The slaves were often reluctant to abandon what they knew well for chancy experiments that did not appear to contribute anything towards their own subsistence. They resisted new work demands that abrogated the prior customs of the plantation and that exceeded those still customary on most neighboring farms. Small wonder that people who had been denied the basics of European education failed to appreciate the rationale underpinning complicated scientific agricultural experiments, the finer points of which usually eluded well-educated white managers.

Washington blamed managers, overseers, and slaves alike for numerous failures. He criticized white supervisors for general incompetence, laziness, lack of managerial skills, and especially for their lack of foresight and preference for short-term profit at the expense of long-run improvement. The slaves almost uniformly failed to adopt his exacting work ethic, instead obviating unwelcome orders through neglect, appropriating his property for their own purposes, and remaining satisfied and sometimes insistent on delivering only that labor and output that regional custom demanded, rather than the dedicated, unremitting, and painstaking efforts he hoped for.

However much the slaves' efforts fell short of Washington's idealized expectations, whatever advances over traditional agriculture that did occur at Mount Vernon in the last quarter of the 18th century could not have happened without a singular transformation among the enslaved workforce. By the close of the 18th century, the men and women who toiled year-round on Mount Vernon's unforgiving soils were far from "ordinary field hands." Through a largely undocumented and largely unrecognized high pressure stint of learning by doing, Mount Vernon's enslaved laborers became some of the most skilled mixed-crop farmers, fishermen, and stock breeders in the region. Unfortunately he and they were tragically enmeshed in a labor system in which the interests of slaves and owner were fundamentally opposed.

THE AGRICULTURAL HISTORY OF THE MOUNT VERNON ESTATE

George Washington began his adult life in more modest circumstances than did most great Chesapeake planters. A younger son of a not especially rich father, Washington inherited but two farms and ten slaves upon his father's death in 1743, and initially had to make a living surveying land for richer men. An unexpected windfall, the inheritance in 1752 of 2,500-acre Mount Vernon from a half brother who died without other heirs, marked the beginning of a notably successful career in farming and estate building. Washington's achievement is particularly remarkable given the frequent interruptions of public service that left little time for active estate management.[2]

The Africans and African-Virginians who came to live at Mount Vernon came from highly varied backgrounds. Since merchants brought relatively few new Africans into the Potomac River, Potomac area planters built up their workforces from varying combinations of African and West Indian laborers purchased in South Potomac, on the Maryland side of that river, or occasionally in the Rappahannock; and a mix of more seasoned Africans and creoles acquired through marriage or inheritance from relatives living in other parts of Virginia and Maryland. Those Washington inherited from his family were probably primarily Africans, as were some of the slaves he later purchased in northern Virginia. Among newly arrived Africans, the majority were likely from Senegambia, since people from that region predominated among arrivals in both South and North Potomac and were the most numerous group brought into the adjoining Rappahannock from the mid-1730s onward. Seasoned African and Virginia-born slaves whom Washington acquired locally would have

50

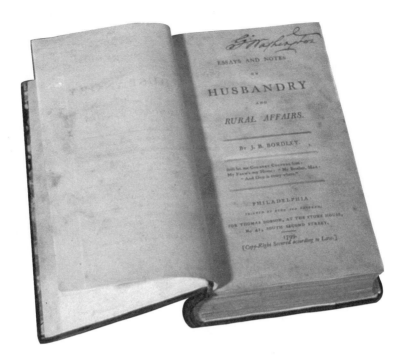

Washington's library included a number of books on agriculture, including this "how to" volume on animal husbandry by James Bordley.

brought particular expertise in land clearing, farm building, and in raising large quantities of oronoco tobacco.[3]

Washington assumed direct supervision of his farms in 1759, the year of his marriage to the propertied widow Martha Custis. This match brought him outright control of Martha's third of her first husband's extensive holdings in York, New Kent, King William, Hanover, and Accomac Counties, and management of the remainder of the Custis lands during the minority of two step-children. Suddenly possessed of large revenues and access to English credit, Washington set about trying to become a rich man. An order to a London factor in the same year for a book entitled *A New System of Agriculture: Or a Speedy Method of Growing Rich* suggests his intentions. Martha's dowry also included a welcome infusion of additional enslaved workers. Between 1754 and 1772, Washington bought additional laborers, especially when estate sales offered bargains. The number of Washington's taxable adult workers in Fairfax County

Washington organized a major fishing operation, which netted some 1.3 million shad and herring in a brief six-week season in the spring. He needed to borrow both boats and slaves from his neighbors to make the venture a profitable one. In some years, he made more money from fishing than he did from any single crop.

(where most of the slaves lived), rose from 29 in 1759, to 76 in 1765, and reached 135 in 1774.

The slaves Martha Custis brought to the marriage came from Parke and Custis family quarters along the York River and on the Eastern Shore, and these workers came from different backgrounds than most Africans brought to the Potomac. Three quarters of Africans transported into the York River in the 18th century came from more southerly and easterly parts of Africa, the Bight of Biafra and West Central Africa. In the 1690s, Daniel Parke II bought slaves carried from the Bight of Biafra; and some of the new Africans John Custis purchased in the 1720s and 1730s probably came from the same region. Laborers whom Custis inherited from his father's Eastern Shore plantations almost certainly included captives from Angola (or their descendants), and Custis probably purchased additional Angolans in the later 1730s. A few others came from the Gold Coast. These laborers were knowledgeable about the cultivation of high quality sweet-scented tobacco and about the more diverse agricultural and craft operations carried out on long established farms.[4]

In the late 1750s, perhaps about a third of the adult laborers on older Custis quarters were Africans. The majority of adults, however, as well as rapidly increasing numbers of children, had been born in Virginia. By the end of the 1760s, when Washington began his first attempts at agricultural improvements, most of the individuals claimed by the Custis estate were Virginia natives. Most were probably of the first generation born in the colony, but some could trace local roots over several generations to African forebears who had arrived a full century earlier.[5] Enslaved creoles, who typically had a better command of English and were more knowledgeable about European ways, were considered better equipped to undertake complex agricultural tasks and plantation crafts. Washington never commented on the differing cultural backgrounds and differing agricultural expertise the slaves he came to control possessed. The varied resources the workers could employ, either to further or to frustrate Washington's plans, were, however, surely a major factor in ensuing successes and failures.

From the outset, Washington showed a strong interest in

53

As a young farmer, Washington pinned his hopes on tobacco, experimenting with five different strains.

improved farming techniques. Certainly there was need, for in the early 1750s Mount Vernon was a "neglected and mediocre plantation." The farm had mostly poor, thin top soils underlaid with a layer of impermeable clay, and much of it was hilly and subject to quick erosion.[6] Washington realized that better pastures were the key to supporting larger herds of cattle and sheep, and thus greater supplies of manure that were essential for increasing yields on naturally unfertile ground, and to keeping draft horses and oxen in condition for plowing and hauling. He began to improve existing meadows by having the slaves grub out brush, ditch low spots, and spread manure. The area's acid soils were inhospitable to non-native grasses, and doubtless many of the experiments Washington ordered in the early 1760s with lucern, clover, trefoil, rye grass, and timothy failed. Meanwhile he sought to augment the supply of animal manure by having the slaves dredge up swamp mud.

He also had the workers begin experimenting with better farm tools, trying out new types of plows, harrows, drills, and rollers. Hoping to improve his stock, Washington purchased English-bred horses and sheep. While concentrating on tobacco, corn, and wheat, he added oats, barley, rye, buckwheat, spelts, turnips, and cotton, and ordered better care of the orchards. Nor did Washington neglect other investment opportunities. He rebuilt his plantation mill, set up a smith shop, and started a fishery on the shores of the Potomac. There were also opportunities to purchase large tracts of western land. By 1763 he had acquired over 9,000 acres in five counties and had set up a farm quarter in Frederick County. He also invested in shares in the Dismal Swamp Company and bought several town lots.

At first, Washington pinned his hopes primarily on tobacco. Since the Custis crops from the York River commanded a premium on the British market, he tried to increase returns by making fine tobacco at Mount Vernon. He had the slaves experiment with five different strains — Frederick, long green, thick joint, Johnson's, and sweet-scented — and with further processing the tobacco by removing stems before packing, seeking to have his crops "Manag'd in every respect in the same manner as the best Tobacco's on James or York River." But the quality of the Fairfax crops remained disappointing. "Certain I am no Person in Virginia takes more pains to make their Tobo. fine than I do and tis hard then I should not be so well rewarded for it."[7]

Washington hoped to garner good prices for tobacco by processing the product to a greater degree than some of his competitors. For instance, he removed all stems before packing the tobacco.

By the early 1760s, Washington found himself in debt from his dealings in tobacco, so he abandoned the product for grains.

Like many other planters who tried to expand operations in the early 1760s, Washington soon found himself in debt. As he explained in 1763, he found his estate under bad management when he returned from the war, and "that[,] besides some purchases of Lands and Negroes I was necessitated to make adjoining me (in order to support the Expences of a large Family), I had Provisions of all kinds to buy for the first two or three years; and my Plantation to stock in short with everything; Buildings to make, and other matters, which swallowed up before I well knew where I was, all the money I got by marriage nay more, brought me in Debt."[8] By 1764 Washington owed his major London factor, Robert Cary, £1800 sterling.

Realizing that he was unlikely to get rich — or even to get out of debt — growing common oronoco, the only strain Potomac River soils could produce, in the mid-1760s Washington decided to abandon tobacco for grains on the Potomac plantations. He reduced the size of the tobacco crop in 1763, ceased culture on most farms in 1765, and had the last crop planted at Dogue Run in 1766. He began to grow more corn but turned to wheat as the main money crop. The conversion took a few years, for it required time to clear the larger acreage wheat required. Washington concentrated on quantity, not quality. He explained to two Alexandria grain traders in 1765: "I may be encouraged indeed to bestow better land to the growth of wheat than old Corn Ground and excited perhaps to a more husbandlike preparation of it but to do either of these is much more expensive than the method now practised and in fact may not be so profitable as the slovenly but easy method of raising it in Corn Ground."[9]

In 1765, a dry year, the slaves made only about 14 bushels of wheat per hand, but within two years they were making over 50 bushels each. This was as much as slaves on major grain estates on Maryland's upper eastern shore produced. Wheat sales jumped from 250 bushels in 1764 to over 6,000 in 1769. And while skimping on land preparation, Washington did put more effort into processing. After the slaves trod out the grain, Washington had them fan the wheat two or three times and then hand riddle it, "a trouble few have the conveniences of doing, and fewer still the Inclination."[10] In the short run the change paid off. Between 1760 and 1764 Washington's gross revenues from tobacco, corn, and wheat averaged £9 1/3 sterling constant value a hand, par for the region. By growing wheat and corn only, within two years gross revenues per laborer rose to over £20 sterling constant value. By 1774 he was able to pay off his debt to Robert Cary.[11]

Washington had greater success with wheat than many of his neighbors because he made substantial changes in plantation operations. He managed to solve the stock food bottleneck that bedeviled others. Slaves' time freed from tobacco could be put into growing more corn. Corn and corn fodder, in combination with swamp draining, creation of water meadows, and continued trials with lucern, timothy, sain foin (a forage herb), clover, and burnet produced enough forage to permit most cultivation to be carried on with plows. Coordinating grass and grain required careful scheduling, since hay was ready to cut at the same time wheat ripened. Washington staggered haymaking, having the slaves cut grass until it was time to harvest wheat, oats, and rye in the last week of June; he then set the haymakers to a second cutting in mid-July. Unencumbered by the need to continually work tobacco, the slaves had more time to put in larger crops of oats, rye, barley, spelts, peas, potatoes, and turnips, as well as for making more cider and growing grapes.

The larger forage crops enabled Washington not only to feed his draft animals, but also to pen more livestock so manure could be efficiently collected. By 1774 the workers were making enough "provender" that he could increase cattle herds, although at this stage there were still too few animals to produce enough manure for all the fields. He experimented as well with marl, and with new tools – drills for sowing seed, a wheat fan, and three Dutch plows. But probably neither fertilizer, tools, nor the still exhausting three-year rotation of corn, wheat, and hay contributed much to increased productivity. Initially, extensive plow culture with adequately fed draft animals was the key to rising output.[12]

This shift from hoe to plow culture profoundly changed work conditions at Mount Vernon as it did on other large Chesapeake plantations. The men (and at Mount Vernon a few strong women) did most of the plowing, harrowing, carting, ditching, and sowing and mowing of grain. Many slave men came to perform a greater variety of tasks that entailed some degree of skill. Slave women

Wheat became Washington's most important crop, and because he experimented with different types and growing techniques, he made higher profits than many of his neighbors.

continued to perform less varied unskilled manual field labor, such as hand hoeing and weeding, and other undesirable chores like building fences, grubbing swamps, cleaning winnowed grain, breaking up new ground too rough or weedy to plow, cleaning stables, and loading and spreading manure, more often without the help of their menfolk, and usually in gangs under the direct supervision of an overseer.[13]

As the Stamp Act crisis unfolded, Washington turned his attentions to plantation self-sufficiency. In 1764 he ordered the slaves to begin growing flax, and the next year added hemp.[14] By 1767 Washington organized a spinning and weaving operation that turned out more than enough fabric for plantation needs. He kept careful records of the costs and returns, and determined that although cloth manufacture would be essential should trade cease, in ordinary circumstances slaves could produce higher returns working the fields.[15] After the war, Washington would continue to have the plantation's wool and small crops of flax and cotton made into cloth; but he returned to purchasing most yardgoods in Alexandria or Philadelphia. To achieve further self-sufficiency, Washington had indentured servants tan leather and make shoes for the slaves. A blacksmith shop served the plantation and neighboring farmers. A team of slave carpenters put up all ordinary buildings, and coopers made casks for flour and fish. Thus the estate was prepared to ride out a trade embargo well before the events of 1774-75 would force the issue.

During the war, Washington left the management of his farms to a relative, Lund Washington, who was experienced in running large plantations. Still, estate revenues dropped drastically.[16] The mill was often shut down as there was little demand for flour. Tenants stopped paying rent. Local men diverted the proceeds of the Custis lands into their own pockets, and Washington was unable to get so much as an accounting until the late 1780s. Winter losses among livestock were unusually heavy; some of the slaves escaped to the British; buildings fell into disrepair; and with improper methods of cultivation, the land took a beating. Writing from camp in 1779, Washington complained, "the devil of anything do I get . . . ten

Washington believed that manure was an exceptional fertilizer, so he constructed a dung repository to facilitate its collection and dispersal in his fields.

thousand pounds will not compensate the losses I might have avoided by being at home, and attending a little to my own concerns."[17]

Lund did manage to sell meat, corn, flour, potatoes, and fish to the army and in 1781 began sending slaves into Alexandria to market meat, fish, and produce. An unintended result was that enhanced chances for trade with the "underling shop keepers" of Alexandria afforded the slaves new opportunities for both "legitimate" and "illegal" exchanges.

After the victory at Yorktown, Washington sought to return to profitable agriculture as quickly as possible. At first prospects seemed bright. He resumed merchant milling in 1782, but the closing of the West Indian market to American shipping forced him to limit post-war flour production. In some years, Washington could make good sales in Norfolk or Alexandria; but in others the flour market was so dull he stopped buying grain for manufacture. Short corn crops in 1785 and 1787 forced him to buy maize, and in 1786 his wheat was "so bad I can neither eat it myself nor sell it to others."[18] When peace came in 1783, Washington considered returning to tobacco but was too uncertain about future markets to switch. By

1789, financial difficulties did induce him to make a limited trial of the old staple.

The credit contraction of 1784-87 hurt Washington deeply. Crop failures reduced farm revenues. Old debts proved impossible to collect, and in some years he was hard-pressed to pay taxes and meet private obligations.[19] Meanwhile he had to accommodate a steady stream of visitors whose presence turned his home into "a well resorted tavern." By 1789 Washington had to borrow £600 to pay debts and cover the expenses of his trip to New York to assume the presidency.

Despite these difficulties, while at home between 1784 and 1788, Washington embarked on a major course of house remodeling, landscaping, and estate improvement. In part he had a position to maintain; in part he truly loved farming. But Washington must also have been either still confident about the nation's future or else determined to do what he could to create confidence by personal example.[20]

As when he returned from the army in 1759, again in 1784 Washington found acute need for change. The full effects of 20 years of extensive clearing and widespread, improper plowing for corn and wheat had taken their toll. "I never ride to my plantations without seeing something which makes me regret having continued so long in the ruinous mode of farming, which we are in," he lamented in 1785.[21] Piecemeal adoption of selected components of English "improving agriculture" had initially raised farm revenues, but some of the new practices were proving more destructive than beneficial in the longer run.[22]

Despite continuing financial pressures, Washington concluded that both long term prosperity and duty to posterity required abandoning schemes for making fast money and instead adopting "a compleat course of husbandry as practiced in the best Farming Counties of England."[23] He opened a correspondence with English agricultural reformer Arthur Young, and began putting Young's ideas into practice. He built a great brick barn with an interior threshing floor following plans Young supplied. He ordered the slaves to begin enclosing carefully laid-out fields with ditches, hedges, and permanent fences. And he engaged an English farmer, James Bloxham, to provide practical advice.

As before the war, meadows and manure were part of the equation. Washington wrote Young in 1787, "very few persons have attended to growing grasses, and connecting cattle with their crops."[24] He ordered slaves to clear new ground for pastures; ditch swamps; make more water meadows; and grub, plow, dung, harrow, and weed existing meadows. He had them try an ever-greater variety of artificial grasses; red, yellow, hop, and sulla clover; orchard, bird, rib, borden, and guinea grasses; timothy; trefoil; lucern; burnet; sain foin; and everlasting and Albany peas. He had seeds saved for the next year's sowing, and experiments made with different methods and rates of seeding. Among the fertilizers tried were dung, plaster, lime, marl, creek mud, and fish heads and guts. By 1786 the slaves raised so much hay that Washington had to hire white laborers to help with a four-week harvest. The object was to "Midas like . . . convert everything . . . into manure, as the first transmutation towards Gold."[25]

Washington remained too practical to entirely neglect his main source of revenue, and he devoted considerable attention to improving wheat. He had little luck with new strains, but found that a combination of early planting and threshing the grain immediately after harvest helped to control Hessian flies. Washington also had the slaves experiment with different methods of plowing and sowing the seed. They tried intensified ground preparation, plowing and harrowing the land two or three times and then rolling in the seed. They tested new kinds of drills, plows, and harrows. He also had them raise minor crops of oats, rye, barley, spelts, buckwheat, peas, and beans, and they continued to grow some cotton and flax. Following the advice of English reformers, Washington expanded acreage in root crops — turnips, Irish and sweet potatoes, carrots, cabbages, parsnips, mangle-wurzel and jerusalem artichokes — for animal and human food. When corn was short, it was costly to feed stock with maize. This squeeze could be avoided by using alternative foods. Root crops were all the more attractive because when grown between rows of corn they could be raised with almost no additional labor.

At the same time Washington sought to limit corn. He was uncertain whether the plant itself was exhausting, or merely the method of cultivation. He was sure that the usual practice of weeding by plowing both across and up and down slopes caused excessive washing of the soil and eventually, deep gullies. The continual throwing up of loosened earth against the corn stalks also built up high ridges, leaving the fields too uneven for easy seeding of subsequent crops of small grains. Consequently Washington had the slaves experiment with new spacings, hoping to grow more corn on fewer acres, and trying to keep the fields level by hoeing and harrowing after plowing.

Other effort went into improving livestock. Washington sought to upgrade his sheep, whose care, much less careful breeding, was neglected during the war. A trial of greater eventual importance was mules, an animal not seriously bred in Virginia before the Revolution. Gifts from the King of Spain and the Marquis de Lafayette provided the donkeys. By trial and error Washington's slaves learned how to breed the jacks to mares, producing draft animals that "perform as much labour, with vastly less feeding than horses."[26]

Not surprisingly, Washington was not entirely successful in quickly transforming his mode of farming. Adequate ground preparation remained a serious bottleneck. Wheat yields could be increased only by inserting a year of fallow between crops of wheat and corn. But this required more work since the fallow fields had to be plowed. In 1787 Washington had the slaves sow the wheat directly on the corn because it was impossible to get the fallow plowed in time.[27] Some of the new crops Washington wanted to include in his rotations, like buckwheat, peas, barley, and clover, often failed because he could not buy good seed. These setbacks wasted labor put into preparing ground that could not be planted, and upset planned rotations. Systematic cropping, Washington learned, required time to implement, and it was difficult to improve the land and to make money at the same time.

In the 1790s Washington remained at Mount Vernon, now ever

more bent on establishing a model operation that other Americans might emulate. His final plans called for abandoning shifting cultivation, instead tilling arable fields indefinitely and maintaining their fertility with manures, soil-enriching vegetable dressings, and complicated crop rotations. Smaller farms were to be consolidated, temporary timber fences eliminated in favor of permanent hedges, and the land improved by English-style rotations. Over six or seven years, fields were shifted through crops of maize and potatoes; wheat or rye; buckwheat, oats or barley; clover or legumes; and manured pasture.[28]

Washington knew he could make greater profits by planting only his best lands in grain; but if he raised full crops, there would be insufficient time and labor to effect the improvements dear to his heart. If Washington occasionally left the impression he was doing little more than surviving hand to mouth, one should not forget that he was among those who adopted a grander style of living than was usual before the Revolution. By the late 1780s, Washington had turned the "Mansion House Farm" into a showplace where appearance was everything and income from crops secondary; and he also maintained a city residence during his two terms as President.[29] His new preoccupation with keeping all the farms "in good order, and everything trim, handsome, and thriving about them" entailed expenses he would not have considered incurring before the Revolution.[30]

Since his public allowance as President was insufficient to cover living expenses in Philadelphia and maintenance costs at Mount Vernon, he sought to finance additional improvements by aggressively collecting debts, raising rents, and by 1799 borrowing from banks to pay for speculative grain purchases. Like many of his fellow planters, Washington also pursued side enterprises such as selling fallen timber for firewood; marketing fish the slaves caught off Mount Vernon; and furnishing urban markets in Alexandria, Georgetown, and Washington D.C. with hay and butter. In 1797 he appended a whisky distillery and hog fattening operation to his mill. He also invested in (or was gifted with) urban property in the District of Columbia and six other Virginia towns, stock in three internal improvement companies and two banks, and U.S. treasury bonds.[31].

Finding an estate manager knowledgeable in either English or Maryland Eastern Shore farming practices and competent to keep the detailed accounts that he needed to evaluate the financial status of multiple enterprises remained a continuing problem. Two Englishmen, a Scot, and a Virginia relative all proved unsatisfactory. Only William Pierce, long-term overseer for the Ringgold family of Kent County, Maryland, performed well but soon left because of bad health. Washington thought even Pierce too inclined to maximize current revenues at the expense of longer-term improvements, but Pierce's combined knowledge of farming methods appropriate to the Chesapeake and long practical experience in supervising slaves produced better results than did less practical or experienced managers.[32] Continued use of run-of-the mill white overseers — men of limited education and little vision — to supervise most of the farms still appeared an unavoidable evil. Since he had abandoned customary cropping schemes, Washington paid his white overseers wages rather than crop shares. Most of the overseers attempted to pursue business as usual, and Washington was continually frustrated by their neglect of his cherished side projects and by their perceived idleness. In 1798, he reduced their wages, since the price of produce was down and taxes had risen.

Records of farm receipts for 1794-1797 show that in these years just over half of Washington's agricultural revenues came from wheat. He sought to make the most of the major crop, sometimes selling the grain outright and sometimes first grinding it into flour, the decision based on the prevailing price differential between wheat and flour. Other grains and root crops added an additional 12 percent to annual revenues, corn, 13 percent, and livestock 19 percent. Given his battle with severe soil erosion, Washington aimed to raise only enough corn to provide bread for the slaves. He wanted to feed the draft animals with oats, turnips, and hay, which required less plowing than corn and hence less loosening of soils. From calculations Washington made in the 1790s, he determined that only with the proceeds of ancillary crops was it possible to make a profit from wheat on worn Potomac farms. From his crop records it appears that the slaves usually made Washington's annual target crop of 20 to 25 barrels of corn per laborer, but that wheat yields sometimes fell short of his target 50 bushels per worker.[33]

Manure and grass were critical to Washington's final plans for improving his land, if not his annual balance sheet; and it was with these that he had the least success. Like most other planters, Washington reserved animal manure for the corn fields; succeeding grain crops depended on this prior fertilization. He also had the slaves make repeated attempts to grow buckwheat as a supplemental vegetable dressing. Turning green manure into the ground required more plowing than could often be accomplished; the buckwheat was never turned in at the right time, and therefore never fully answered expectations. In the end, Washington resorted to using creek mud for manure.

Planned crop rotations similarly called for changes in cultivation methods. The various schedules he contemplated required between 855 and 1055 person days of plowing on each of his four farms. Inability to get the plowing done early threatened the rotations altogether, and inadequate ground preparation lowered grain yields. Although he possessed more laborers than all but a handful of other planters, Washington still had too few to meet peak season requirements. In some measure, animals — especially mules — supplemented the efforts of more expensive human workers. In 1793, Washington used 54 work horses and 12 mules at Mount Vernon; by 1799, when drivers and plowmen had learned how to train them, there were 42 working mules on the farms and but 20 work horses.[34]

Better livestock management remained essential too, both for producing supplemental income and for providing adequate supplies of fertilizer. Washington worked to breed better mules and improve the quality of the sheep and cattle. He tried to find the cheapest methods for fattening cattle and hogs for market (he had the slaves try various penning and feeding schemes that utilized secondary crops such as potatoes), better ways to carry cattle and sheep through the winter (rigorous culling of existing herds in the fall and use of turnips as winter food), and the most economical means of managing draft animals (substituting mules for horses and giving no extra food to non-working horses and oxen). This is another instance where Washington has been accorded all the credit. Yet it was the slaves who learned through practical experience how to turn notoriously recalcitrant creatures into reliable and efficient draft animals and to tend the more tender breeds of cattle and sheep.

LABOR MANAGEMENT AT MOUNT VERNON

Did Washington devise new ways of managing labor as well as land? Before the Revolution, his strategies were in many ways similar to those of the better-documented, ever-demanding, and frequently irascible Landon Carter. Most Mount Vernon workers labored in the fields in gangs, and were usually directed by a white overseer. In order to raise efficiency, Washington divided his slaves into work groups of similar abilities. By the 1780s most farms had two or more gangs divided according to gender and age. Washington had every intention of "making those who are to execute it do what is reasonable and proper without suffering so much time to be spent in the house, under pretence of sickness; which is, in many cases, no other than the effect of Night walking and fatigue."[35] Devising ways to keep up a fast work pace concerned Washington as much as Carter. But Washington, unlike Carter, found physical discipline distasteful, if occasionally necessary. After the war, Washington did allow enslaved artisans to pursue their crafts with considerable independence, and in the 1780s took the unusual step of appointing three black overseers — Davy at River Plantation, Morris at Dogue Run, and Will at Muddy Hole. However, on the whole, close regulation and not autonomy were the rule.

Before the Revolution, Washington's overseers and managers, if not Washington himself, had to meet some different challenges from those that bedeviled Carter. Separating the dower slaves allotted to Martha Washington from their extended southern Virginia kin and uprooting them from homes on the Custis quarters inflicted hardships and likely stiffened resistance among those compelled to move. In addition, transplanting them to quarters where unfamiliar plantation customs shaped expectations about kinds and intensity of work, allowances, privileges, and discipline, may at first have

Rotation for a Farm of Six fields.

Number of the Fields	1797.	1798.	1799.	1800.	1801.	1802.
1.	Corn & Potatoes	Wheat Rye or &c.	Buck wheat or &c.	Oats or barley with Clover	Clover or Pulse	Pasture & manure
2.	Pasture & manure	Corn & Pota.º	Wheat Rye or &c.	Buck wheat or &c.	Oats or barley with Clover	Clover or Pulse
3.	Clover or Pulse	Pasture & manure	Corn & Pota.º	Wheat Rye or &c.	Buck wheat or &c.	Oats or barley with Clover
4.	Oats or barley with Clover	Clover or Pulse	Pasture & manure	Corn & Pota.º	Wheat Rye or &c.	Buck wheat or &c.
5.	Buck wheat or &c.	Oats barley with Clover	Clover or Pulse	Pasture & manure	Corn & Pota.º	Wheat Rye or &c.
6.	Wheat Rye or &c.	Buck wheat or &c.	Oats or barley with Clover	Clover or Pulse	Pasture & manure	Corn & Pota.º

A farm containing 100 acres, gives six fields of 16 acres each, & leaves 4 acres for the houses, garden &c. . . . the said farm annually; these at a very moderate estimate will produce as follow.—

16 acres in Indian Corn at 12 bush.ˢ is 192 bush.ˢ a 3/ is £ 28. 16
Same in Potatoes — do. .... do. .... 2/ — 19. 4
16 acres Wheat ... — 10 .... 160 — 6/ .. 48 .
16 acres Buck wheat .. — 10 .... 160 — 2/ .. 16 .
16 acres Oats .... 15 ... 240 — 2/6. 30 —
16 acres Clover or Vegetables .. uncertain ....

Total besides Clover or &c. .... £ 142. 0 —
Rent of 100 acres at a dollar & half pr. acre, — 45. 0 —
Remains for the Tenant 97

In England, where taxes & rents are both high, it is estimated that if every thing which is raised on the farm will sell for three times the rent, that the farmer is in eligible circumstances.— One third pays the rent — another third the taxes, & all other incidental expenses of the farm and the remaining third is applied to whatever purposes the farmer may chuse. The above principles & proportions, apply equally to large & small farms.

Washington worked diligently to develop a successful plan for crop rotation, which included crops like corn and wheat, but also clover, which would often be plowed under to reinvigorate the soil.

undercut the dower slaves' ability to resist unfavorable changes by appealing to past practice. Persuading or forcing them to work efficiently with resident Africans who spoke different languages and drew on different cultural backgrounds, as well as with Northern Neck creoles who had better established local ties, was likely not accomplished without some friction.

With time, new "customs of the plantation" were negotiated, increasing the bargaining power of all the laborers in resisting innovations that altered work routines or further curtailed leisure. Members of the different groups accommodated whatever differences that may initially have divided them, and forged more cohesive communal bonds. Northern Neck and former southern Virginia slaves intermarried and raised families with complex ties to others living on the estate and on adjoining plantations. The workers through whom Washington sought to effect agricultural change in the 1790s were almost entirely creoles with well established local connections and a native's familiarity with the locality.

Only after further study of the slaves' individual and family histories can we tell the story from their perspective. What were the skills with which they arrived and which they acquired over time? To what extent did the kinds of agricultural expertise the slaves' possessed when they became part of Washington's estate influence his subsequent agricultural plans and contribute to the overall successes of the estate? To what extent could they use established plantation custom to mitigate increased work requirements and alternations in provisions? What aspects of improved agriculture did the slaves accept and master, and what aspects did they resist or refuse to adopt? Why did they adopt some new ways and reject others? What was the role of the enslaved overseers in the successful implementation of new crops, livestock, and agricultural techniques? In perpetuating some aspects of traditional agriculture? How did ordinary field workers define their roles and responsibilities as involuntary participants in an unusually ambitious course of experimental agriculture? Where did they draw the line between grudging adaptation and concerted resistance? These are issues that can and must be addressed in developing a comprehensive history of slavery and agriculture at Mount Vernon.

Washington's major innovations in labor management involved more careful planning and fuller utilization of the whole work force. He expected managers and overseers to anticipate and overcome temporary labor shortages with a due application of "sober, settled work", rather than reacting at the last minute with a poorly-organized speedup. Since most of his farms were adjacent to one another, Washington was in a better position than most planters to shift workers from one unit to another with little loss of time.

In the late 1780s, Washington would pay increasing attention to this careful allocation of labor. In 1785, he informed a new manager, Augustine Washington: "I am resolved that an account of the stock and every occurrence that happens in the course of the week shall be minutely detailed to me every Saturday. Matters cannot go much out of sorts in that time without a seasonable remedy."[36] Augustine's weekly reports for the farms, accompanied by Sally Fairfax's reports on domestic workers, enabled Washington to assess all tasks accomplished in terms of man and woman days of labor.[37] It was not the details themselves that interested him, but rather the way they combined to supply a fuller picture of the entire operation: "Unless the different kinds of business which occupy the labourers of every Plantation, or Farm, can be brought into one view, and seen in time; and a due proportion of work is exacted from the hands, that are to perform it, the different kinds of work will forever be interfering with, and in the way of each other."[38] Washington was finding the administrative skills essential for running an army equally useful for running a plantation. "Contrivance in the arrangement of business, and a happy nack in having it executed by an observance of method; are the distinguishing characteristics of a good Manager."[39]

Labor management presented an increasing dilemma in the 1790s. Washington became almost obsessed with curtailing thefts and with extracting maximum work effort, requiring that even disabled slaves perform sedentary chores such as knitting, and that the able-bodied should labor diligently whenever weather, daylight, and strength permitted.[40] He doggedly pursued slaves who ran away, deciding it was unfair to those remaining to allow any to escape; and he considered selling off thieves and runaways to maintain plantation discipline. The relatively few Mount Vernon men and women who chose to flee helped to convince Washington that slavery had no future in Virginia.

Richard Parkinson reported that "it was the sense of all his neighbours that he treated [his slaves] . . . with more severity than any other man," carefully weighing rations to make certain that allowances were not exceeded; "he probably knew what they cost [for maintenance] to a fraction."[41] Such aggressive cost containment was becoming common practice for most large planters, but Washington's treatment of his slaves became a political as well as a personal issue. For example, he attempted to make minor changes in rations in 1793, substituting a struck peck of sifted corn meal for the former allotment of a heaped peck, unsifted. "Since the meal has been given to them sifted, and a struck peck only, of it, there has been eternal complaints; which I have suspected arose as much from the want of the husks to feed their fowls, as from any other cause, 'till Davy [a slave overseer] assured me that what his people received was not sufficient, and that to his certain knowledge several of them would often be without a mouthful for a day, and (if they did not eke it out) sometimes two days." Washington quickly returned to the usual ration: "in most explicit language I desire they may have plenty: for I will not have my feelings again hurt with Complaints of this sort, nor lye under the imputation of starving my negros and thereby driving them to the necessity of thieving to supply the deficiency. To prevent waste or embezzlement is the only inducement to allowancing of them at all, for if, instead of a peck they could eat a bushel of meal a week fairly, and required it, I would not withhold or begrudge it them."[42]

Although Washington was better acquainted with his vast western holdings (6,700 acres in Western Virginia, 33,000 acres in present-day West Virginia, and 8,000 acres in Kentucky and the Northwest Territory) than many absentee owners, he planned no future there for himself or his heirs, except as rentiers. Nor did he consider sending some slaves to develop these western lands. Age, political responsibilities, lack of direct heirs, and a growing distaste for chattel slavery all combined to confine his personal vision to tidewater Virginia. He did work to increase rental income from western lands, preferring to take payment in wheat rather than cash, as he considered grain a more certain and stable commodity than money. And he continued to convert early long-term leases into shorter-term contracts so that he could more easily evict unsatisfactory tenants and raise rents as land values increased.

Many of Washington's contemporaries with estates of similar size abandoned or did not seek major political careers after the Revolution, instead devoting full time to managing their estates. Others who became political leaders had difficulty juggling official careers and planting; they often neglected their farms and spent beyond their incomes. Although many of his experiments proved disappointing and his frequent absences from Mount Vernon prevented the systematic execution of more ambitious schemes, Washington's ability to plan far ahead and his grasp of the inter-relationships of various parts of his operations was exceptional. Washington was in the forefront of new styles of plantation management with his strict accounting practices, efforts to control costs, explicit equation of time with money, and his insistence that "system to all things is the soul of business."[43] As he lavished more effort and money upon the land, Washington began to gauge his performance as a farmer more by English than by American standards. Unlike almost all his contemporaries, his concern shifted from yields *per laborer* to yields *per acre*.

Had Washington put economic profit above all else, he should have followed up changes in crop mix and cultivation techniques by reducing the number of slaves at Mount Vernon, because mixed grain farming required fewer hands, especially fewer women and children, than did tobacco culture. Indeed, Washington knew he had many more slaves than he could efficiently employ on the Mount Vernon complex, and had he had direct heirs, he might have made other decisions to perpetuate family fortunes. Most other similarly-situated slave owners would either have sent at least half of their slaves to western Virginia to develop new plantations, or have begun selling off or hiring out some of the unneeded workers. Nearing the end of his life, unlike most of his fellow great planters, Washington could not bring himself to hire out, move, or sell any slaves, and eventually decided to free all the bonds people he owned outright at death.[44]

What Washington could not do was to reconcile his vision of Mount Vernon as a model improved estate with the fundamentally opposed interests of the people he expected to implement his plans. They strenuously resisted the increased work load that permanently enclosed fields, meadows, and complicated crop rotations entailed. (So too did most of the overseers who were disinclined either to work harder themselves or to try to force slaves to do more work than was customary on other farms in the area.) The Mount Vernon slaves had ample reason for failing to respond enthusiastically to Washington's demand that they sacrifice what little leisure time they could command for the betterment of a new nation in which they had no personal stake.

NOTES

1. Jackson T. Main, "The One Hundred," *William and Mary Quarterly* 3d ser., 11 (1954), 354-84, provides a ranking of the largest Virginia slave holders in 1787-88.

2. The most complete biography is Douglas Southall Freeman, *George Washington, A Biography*, 7 vols. (New York, 1949-1957). Volumes one through three discuss Washington's early career and debt problems. This essay draws heavily on my analysis of Washington in the overall context of large Chesapeake planters in a manuscript in progress, "'To Labour for Profit': Plantation Management in the Chesapeake, 1620-1820."

3. For the slave trade of Virginia's South Potomac Naval District see Lorena S. Walsh, "The Chesapeake Slave Trade: Regional Patterns, African Origins, and Some Implications," *William and Mary Quarterly*, 3d ser., 58 (2001), 139-70, and Donald M. Sweig, "The Importation of African Slaves to the Potomac River, 1732-1772," *ibid*, 42 (1985), 507-24. The main features of Potomac basin agriculture are discussed in Walsh, "Summing the Parts: Implications for Estimating Chesapeake Output and Income Subregionally," *Ibid.*, 56 (1999), 53-94. On Washington's probable purchase of Africans from Senegambia see Sweig, "Importation of African Slaves," 519-21, and David Eltis, Stephen D.

Behrendt, David Richardson, and Herbert S. Klein, *The Trans-Atlantic Slave Trade: A Database on CD-Rom* (Cambridge, 1999), ship ID no. 90773. New Africans Washington bought in Maryland in 1759 may have been brought from either Senegambia or the Gold Coast. Sweig, "Importation of African Slaves," 518-19, and Eltis, et al., *The Trans-Atlantic Slave Trade Database*, ship ID nos. 90710 and 90763.

4. Walsh, "The Chesapeake Slave Trade," and Walsh, "Summing the Parts." Inventories of the slaves in the Custis estate are published in Joseph E. Fields, comp., *"Worthy Partner": The Papers of Martha Washington* (Westport, Conn., 1994), 61-76, 105-108. For Angolans on the eastern shore see T. H. Breen and Stephen Innes, *"Myne Owne Ground": Race and Freedom on Virginia's Eastern Shore, 1640-1676* (New York, 1980), 17, 71, 130n-131n. For African regional origins of some of the Custis slaves see York County, Virginia, Deeds, Wills, and Orders, 10, 24 (microfilm, Library of Virginia), and Eltis, et al., *Trans-Atlantic Slave Trade Database*, ship ID no. 14913, and John Custis to [Boll and Dee], 1721, John Custis Letterbook, 1717-1741, Library of Congress, and Eltis, et al., *Trans-Atlantic Slave Trade Database*, ship ID no. 75809.

5. Lorena S. Walsh, *From Calabar to Carter's Grove: The History of a Virginia Slave Community* (Charlottesville, 1997), 142-43, 300-301.

6. Raymond George Peterson, Jr., "George Washington, Capitalistic Farmer: A Documentary Study of Washington's Business Activities and Sources of His Wealth" (Ph.D. diss., Ohio State University, 1970), chap. 1. Primary sources consulted are John C. Fitzpatrick, ed., *The Writings of George Washington from the Original Manuscript Sources, 1745-1799*, 39 vols. (Washington, D.C., 1931-1944); Ledgers A and B, 1750-1793, MS, Library of Congress, microfilm CW-M 89.2, Colonial Williamsburg Foundation Library; W. W. Abbot et al., eds., *The Papers of George Washington*, 45 vols. to date (Charlottesville, Va., 1976-), *The Diaries of George Washington*, 1-5; Washington Family Papers, Additional, container 26, including Battaile Muse Account, 1785-90, Rentals due George Washington, 1788-90, Tobias Lear Accounts 1789-91, and Journal of Work on Plantations [1786-87], MSS, Library of Congress.

7. *Writings*, 2, 327-36, 356-57.

8. *Ibid.*, 396-98.

9. *Ibid.*, 422-23. Cf. *The Journal of Nicholas Cresswell, 1774-77* (Port Washington, N.Y., 1968), 198, on slovenly ground preparation for wheat.

10. Cresswell, *Journal*, 444-53.

11. Since Washington changed his method of calculating overseers' shares in the later 1760s, consistent yields and revenues per slave are difficult to calculate. He surely continued to gross at least £20 per worker into the early 1770s, and perhaps did better. In addition, Washington inherited a share of his step-daughter, Patsy Custis's estate, which he used to help pay off his debts. Washington also continued a course of investment in real estate and in commercial ventures in the late 1760s and early 1770s. By 1771 he paid quit rents on 12,000 acres and was beginning to lease western lands to tenants. New

acquisitions included more town lots, and lands in North Carolina, Pennsylvania, and along the Ohio River. In 1770 he built a merchant mill and by the next year was turning his own wheat as well as grain purchased from others into flour. This he sold in Norfolk and Alexandria or else shipped to the West Indies or Madeira. Investment in the grain trade also led Washington to purchase shares in several ships. Expansion of his fishery made this too an important commercial venture. The Mount Vernon slaves caught more than enough fish to supply local needs, and Washington shipped surpluses to Philadelphia and to the West Indies.

12. John Mercer of Marlboro, Stafford County, also attempted to switch to grain culture in 1766 in order to make money by brewing and selling beer on a large scale. Instead of phasing in the changes, he tried to do everything in one year and had to purchase 40 additional slaves "to enable me to make Grain sufficient to carry on my brewery with my own hands." Mercer's expectations as well as those of some other area planters who advised him were unrealistic. Mercer expected to produce 10,000 bushels of barley a year, but in fact could make only 2,000. He had heard that Washington had made 8,000 bushels of wheat with 20 hands in 1766. This implies an impossible output of 400 bushels a hand; the highest yield per laborer found in any sources for this period is 150 bushels, and Washington's yield in that year was about 50 bushels per laborer. Not surprisingly, Mercer's scheme was a total, very expensive failure. *George Mercer Papers Relating to the Ohio Company of Virginia, Lois Mulkearn,* ed. (Pittsburgh, 1954), 189-98.

13. Lois Green Carr and Lorena S. Walsh, "Economic Diversification and Labor Organization in the Chesapeake, 1650-1820," in *Work and Labor in Early America, ed. Stephen Innes* (Charlottesville, 1988), 144-188.

14. Washington toyed briefly with the idea of producing hemp and flax for export, but decided that fibers would make poor staples given low prices in Europe and indifferent success with hemp. Other planters had similar experiences with hemp. In 1764 Thomas Jones, Sr., after observing the fatal effects of drought on his hemp crop, decided "for my Part I do not intend to enter deeply into it, until I see the success they [others] meet with." no. 2737, Jones Family Papers, MS, Library of Congress. John Baylor told John Backhouse in the same year that he was trying a little hemp — whose culture he did not understand — and anticipated that the crop would succeed only if high bounties were offered. 3 September 1764, John Baylor Letterbook, 1757-65, photostat, Colonial Williamsburg Foundation Library. William Beverley thought hemp entailed insuperable difficulties and was likely to end in failure, as had indigo culture a few years before. Letter to John Bland, n.d. [1764 or 65], Robert Beverley Letterbook, 1761-1793, MS, Library of Congress, microfilm CW M-3, Colonial Williamsburg Foundation Library.

15. Some records of Washington's weaving business are reproduced in Ulrich B. Phillips, ed., *Plantation and Frontier, Documents: 1649-1863,* 2 vols. (Cleveland, 1909) II, 319-25.

16. Lund Washington Account Book, 1762-84, MS, U.S. Naval Academy Museum, microfilm CW-M 1201, Colonial Williamsburg Foundation Library. Wartime crop allocations are unclear, since Lund stopped recording totals in 1776 when he began working for a salary rather than for a share of the crops. Grain production was cut back to some extent, but the slaves still made some surpluses. Seizing what few chances for trade remained, Washington invested in shares in a privateer, and received some income from successful runs to the West Indies by ships in which he had an interest.

17. *Writings*, 14, 431-32.

18. *Ibid.*, 29, 158-62.

19. In 1784 Washington lamented, "Those who owed me, for the most part, took advantage of the depreciation and paid me off with six pence in the pound. Those to whom I was indebted, I have yet to pay, without other means, if they will not wait, than selling part of my Estate; or distressing those who were too honest to take advantage of the tender Laws to quit scores with me." *Ibid.*, 27, 345-46.

20. The state of the farms in the late 1780s is described in Louis B. Wright and Marion Tinling, eds., *Quebec to Carolina in 1785-1786 Being the Travel Diary and Observations of Robert Hunter, Jr., a Young Merchant of London* (San Marino, Calif., 1943), 192-97, and in J. P. Brissot de Warville, *New Travels in the United States of America, 1788*, trans. Mara Soceanu Vamos, and ed. Durand Echeveria (Paris, 1791; Cambridge, Mass., 1964), 343.

21. *Writings*, 28, 310-14.

22. The villain was not, as has been sometimes suggested, tobacco, but grain. As Washington informed agricultural reformer John Beale Bordley, "that the system (if it deserves the appellation of one) of Corn, Wheat, hay; has been injurious, and if continued would prove ruinous to our lands, I believe no one who has attended to the ravages which have been produced by it in our fields, is at a loss to decide." *Ibid.*, 29, 47-52.

23. *Ibid.*, 28, 182-88.

24. *Ibid.*, 29, 296-300.

25. *Ibid.*, 28, 182-88.

26. *Ibid*, 30, 150-54.

27. J. Hector St. John de Crèvecoeur in *Sketches of Eighteenth-Century America* (republished New York, 1981), 141, commented on the difficulty all colonial farmers faced in getting wheat fallows plowed in time.

28. Sources for the 1790s include *Writings*, vols. 30-37; General Business Account Book, 6 January 1794-7 November 1796, MS, Library of Congress; and Peterson, "George Washington, Capitalistic Farmer."

29. Robert Carter chose to live in similar style at Nomini Hall in the 1780s, and great planters like John Tayloe and Edward Lloyd made similar choices in the 1790s.

30. *Writings*, 32, 177-85; 33, 110-12.

31. *Writings*, 35, 480-82; 37, 275-303.

32. Pierce's earlier experiences as overseer for the Ringgolds is documented in the Galloway-Maxey-Markoe Papers, MS, Library of Congress.

33. Richard Parkinson, in *A Tour in America in 1798, 1799, and 1800*, 2 vols. (London, 1805), 1:6-8, 52-53, 423-25, provides an unflattering description of Washington's farming methods. He stated that Washington made only 2 to 3 bushels of wheat per acre; this may be an exaggeration, but corroborates other evidence for poor wheat yields at Mt. Vernon.

34. Cf. Parkinson, *A Tour in America*, 224.

35. *Writings*, 29, 264-66.

36. *Ibid.*, 28, 363-64.

37. Journal of Work, Washington Additional Papers.

38. *Writings*, 29, 264-66.

39. *Ibid.*

40. Cf. Lee's essay in this volume.

41. *A Tour in America*, 418, 454.

42. *Writings*, 32, 470-77, 434-38; Lorena S. Walsh, "Work and Resistance in the New Republic: The Case of the Chesapeake, 1770-1820" in *From Chattel Slaves to Wage Slaves: The Dynamics of Labour Bargaining in the Americas*, ed. Mary Turner (London, 1995), 97-122, discusses slave treatment as a political issue.

43. *Writings*, 36:110-14. Cf. 37, 459-63. Cf. also John Taylor, "Time constitutes profit or loss in agriculture," in *Arator, Being a Series of Agricultural Essays, Practical and Political: in Sixty-Four Numbers*, M.E. Bradford, ed., (1818; Indianapolis, 1977), 312.

44. For overall developments see Carr and Walsh, "Economic Diversification and Labor Organization"; Lorena S. Walsh, "Plantation Management in the Chesapeake, 1620-1820," *Journal of Economic History*, 49 (1989), 393-406; and Lorena S. Walsh, "Slave Life, Slave Society, and Tobacco Production in the Tidewater Chesapeake," in *Cultivation and Culture: Labor and the Shaping of Slave Life in the Americas*, ed. Ira Berlin and Philip Morgan (Charlottesville, 1993), 170-99.

Washington worked diligently to control his slaves during the workday, but even in the most personal aspects of their lives, his slaves were never free of his ultimate control.

"They Appear to Live Comfortable Together" Private Lives of the Mount Vernon Slaves

Mary V. Thompson

The hours when they were not working for their master must have been very precious to the members of Mount Vernon's enslaved community, for it was then that they had the time and, to a great extent, the freedom to pursue their own interests and exercise some measure of control over their own lives. Slaves living on George Washington's outlying farms may have had even more freedom in their private lives than those at the Mansion House, where personal servants had to be available well into the evening, under the close and almost constant supervision of the master and his family. Surviving correspondence between Washington and his managers, financial records, and descriptions left by 18th-century visitors suggest that slaves used their free time for building families, for recreation, and to enhance their overall economic position. It is just as evident, however, that even in their "free time" and in the most personal aspects of their lives, Washington's slaves were never free of his ultimate control.

MARRIAGE

Marriage was a basic building block of the slave community at Mount Vernon in the 18th century, as it was throughout the Chesapeake area. This was possible because here, in stark contrast with slave systems elsewhere in the Americas, the numbers of males and females in the slave population were roughly equal. At Mount Vernon, for instance, there were 148 males and 168 females in 1799, when the enslaved population reached its highest point. A list made that summer, several months before George Washington's death, indicates that roughly two-thirds of the plantation's adult slaves were married. While they were neither recognized nor protected by the legal system, these marriages were acknowledged by both the slave community and the Washingtons. George Washington once referred to marriage as "the most interesting event of one's life, the

79

foundation of happiness or misery."[1] For a slave, it was all of that, plus the opportunity to exercise choice in a life that afforded little personal control over such basic issues as occupation, housing, clothing, and the ability to travel.

A couple planning to marry seem to have first needed permission from George Washington, at least if they lived on different plantations. A long-distance marriage would necessitate a certain amount of traveling back and forth between plantations. Getting permission from a master would have been in keeping with a Virginia law that stated that slaves could not travel away from home without a pass or letter of authorization from a master, employer, or overseer.[2] Several months before his death in 1799, George Washington wrote about the marriage of one of his house servants to a young woman belonging to a neighbor: "Sometime ago the Servant who waits upon me, Christopher (calling himself Christopher Sheels) asked my permission to marry a mulatto girl belonging to you." He commented that since Christopher had "behaved as well as servants usually do" and the prospective bride was "well spoken of, . . . I told him I had no objection to the union, provided your consent (which was necessary) could be obtained."[3] There is no way to know at this point if Washington's permission was required for all marriages on the plantation. There is also no evidence for the type of ceremony or ritual, if one existed, that may have publicly, if not legally, united a couple in the eyes of their community.

George Washington not only recognized but also respected the marriage and family relationships of his enslaved workers. In a letter written several years after the Revolution, he wrote, "it is . . . against my inclination . . . to hurt the feelings of those unhappy people by a separation of man and wife, or of families."[4] One of Washington's primary concerns at the end of his life was that freeing his slaves would lead to the dissolution of slave families, for there had been considerable intermarriage over a period of forty years between his slaves and those of Mrs. Washington, who were actually part of her first husband's estate and could not be freed by her.[5]

Some of the best evidence for the strength of these marriages comes from incidents that threatened to tear them apart. To give just one example, during the Revolution, George Washington's mother asked that a Mount Vernon slave named Silla be sent to her in Fredericksburg. The estate was then being managed by a cousin, Lund Washington, who noted that he would comply with the request, but that Silla would probably be unwilling to go because of her attachment to her husband, a cooper named Jack, with whom she appeared to "live comfortable together." Lund was "very sorry" about separating the two, but his distress was nothing compared to the pain felt by Jack, who "cries and begs, saying he had rather be hanged than separated."[6] Inclement weather may have postponed Silla's departure for a time. In the last communication to mention this incident, Lund blamed "the badness of the weather" for not sending her sooner and mentioned once more how "much distressed" Jack and Silla were about being parted.[7] A sizable break in the correspondence between Lund and his cousin at this point prevents our knowing how the situation was resolved.

Human nature being what it is, however, not every slave marriage was stable or a source of comfort. In February 1795, a young woman at River Farm named Fanny was "Laid up" for an entire six-day work week, because she had been "badly beat" by her husband Ben, who was owned by a Mr. Fowler.[8] George Washington was so incensed that he forbid Ben from returning to Mount Vernon and ordered him whipped if he disobeyed. Four years later Fanny had remarried, once again to a slave living off the plantation.[9]

Fanny's situation illustrates something that was probably a significant stress factor in slave marriages — distance. Of the 96 married slaves on Washington's five farms in 1799, only 36 lived in the same household as their spouse and children. Another 38 had spouses living on one of Washington's other farms, a situation resulting primarily from work assignments. Slaves were generally housed on the farm where they worked because "commuting" from one farm to work on another would have cost dearly in both lost work and time. Other Mount Vernon slaves, 22 in fact, had like Fanny married people belonging to other plantations. There is no indication that marriages were arranged, so, in order for these couples to meet and form the attachments that would eventually lead

Edward Savage's famous portrait of the Washington Family includes an unidentified slave.

to marriage, there must have been a certain degree of freedom for slaves to travel from farm to farm within the plantation or to the plantations of other owners, as well as occasions for socializing.[10]

While husbands and wives might often be separated because of their jobs, the overall pattern of their lives was fairly constant. For example, of the 59 adult slaves living at the Mansion House Farm in 1799, 78 percent had been living on that site for at least 13 years. Although the nature of the work on the four outlying farms was quite different from the "Home House," a similar stability of population prevailed. At the end of George Washington's life, 83 percent of the adult slaves at Dogue Run had lived there since 1786, as had 71 percent of the adults at River Farm, and 79 percent at Muddy Hole. At Union Farm, not counting 38 slaves who were rented from a neighbor, 16 of the 17 adult slaves had been living there since at least 1786.[11] This continuity was a major factor leading to the formation of an African-American community at Mount Vernon made up of extended, multi-generational families. It also enabled the development of long-term friendships. Together, these two types of stable relationships would go a long way toward creating a support network for individuals living within the boundaries of slavery, an institution into which instability and tenuousness were built as part of the system.

With Sunday being the weekly day off for everyone except possibly house servants, the individuals involved in these long-distance marriages could see one another on Saturday night and during the day on Sunday, as well as during other holidays, such as Christmas and Easter, throughout the year. The slaves at Mount Vernon both were visited by their spouses and paid visits to them, although such arrangements could always be curtailed at the desire of a master. For example, Washington complained in the fall of 1769 that a neighbor had "under frivolous pretenses forbid two or three of my People who had Wives in his Family from coming there again."[12] Many years later during the presidency, concerned that affairs at Mount Vernon were getting out of control during his absence, Washington ordered his farm manager to "absolutely forbid the Slaves of others resorting to the Mansion House; such only excepted as have wives or husbands there, or such as you may particularly license from a knowledge of their being honest and well disposed." After giving them a warning, all others were to be punished "whensoever you shall find them transgressing these orders."[13]

Renowned artist Eastman Johnson created this rare depiction of a slave working in the servant's hall at Mount Vernon.

The marriages of the Mount Vernon slaves produced a large number of children and the population on the estate increased dramatically, from about 50 slaves in 1759 to more than 300 in 1799. In the latter year, on Washington's four outlying farms the average age of the slave population was slightly less than 21 years. Only about nine percent of the people were 60 years old or more, while 58 percent were under the age of 19. Almost 35 percent were younger than nine, confirming a description recorded by a French visitor to Mount Vernon: "These unfortunates [the slaves] reproduce freely, and their number is increasing . . . these shacks swarm with pickaninnies in rags that our own beggars would scorn to wear."[14] Over the years a number of very large, multi-generational extended families developed, another factor that led to the creation of a real community among the slaves of Washington's five farms and the surrounding neighborhood. Looking at just one family as an example, in 1799, head carpenter Isaac and his wife Kitty, who was a milkmaid, had nine daughters ranging in age from twenty-seven to six. Through the marriages of four of the girls, Isaac and Kitty's family was linked to slaves at Washington's mill, Tobias Lear's Walnut Tree Farm, and possibly to others at Washington's Ferry Farm. These marriages had also given Isaac and Kitty three grandchildren.

When it came time to give birth and as they recuperated afterwards, enslaved women at Mount Vernon might be attended by either a white midwife or by another slave woman. For instance, Lynna at Dogue Run Farm had a difficult time during and after the birth of her son in February 1793. Two slave women, Matilda and Moll, took care of her for two days about the time the baby was born; a little over a month later, Moll was off from her regular duties for an entire week to look after Lynna, whose baby had died shortly after birth.[15] A number of the midwives mentioned in Washington's financial accounts were the wives of white men who were working for him.[16] The midwife might also be another slave woman, either from Mount Vernon or a neighboring plantation. In the summer of 1794,

Kate from Muddy Hole Farm, the wife of an enslaved overseer, approached Washington to request that she be given the job of "Granny" for the other slave women. Washington asked his farm manager to look into Kate's credentials and, if all was satisfactory, to entrust the business to her.[17] In particularly difficult cases, a white male doctor, frequently Washington's old comrade Dr. James Craik, might be brought in to assist.[18] Rum was routinely sent from the storehouse near the Mansion for the use of "women in childbed," but it is unclear whether it was used as an anesthetic during labor, was thought to be a restorative afterwards, or was a reward for a job well done.[19]

The low value placed on this new little life can be seen in an entry from Dogue Run Farm in which the overseer recorded the weekly changes in the population as: "Increase 9 Lambs & 1 male child of Lynnas Decrease 1 male Child of Charitys & 2 Cows & Calves sent to Mansion House."[20] After the birth, the mother was generally given three to five weeks off to recover.[21] Infants probably accompanied their mothers to their work sites, at least while they were still being nursed and before they became too active to either happily stay on a blanket near where she was working or be carried on her back.[22]

A mother would be issued her new blanket for the year at the time her baby was born.[23] One surviving letter suggests that if the baby lived, the mother might also receive a new blanket for herself at the time of the fall distribution, but if it died, she would just have the one given at the time of the birth.[24] Rewarding mothers, in essence, with an extra blanket may have been a means of increasing the survival rate for babies. In addition to the blanket, baby clothes of "Slazy White Linnen" were also issued, although there is no indication of how many garments each baby would receive.[25]

It is not known whether a child's family or the Washingtons chose its name, but if Mount Vernon followed the typical pattern on other plantations, parents or other relatives probably determined what to call their baby.[26] An extensive pool of names, drawn from a wide range of sources, was used on the estate over the years. About half of the names are of English origin, while another third are

Winslow Homer's 1861 watercolor of the Mount Vernon Mansion shows an African American in the shadows. It is unknown whether the person was one of Washington's former slaves.

biblical. Only a tiny fraction of the names, fewer than one percent, appear on the surface to have been African. It may be, however, that a number of common slave names that appear to be of European derivation were actually African names written down the way masters understood them or transposed to their closest-sounding English equivalent.[27] If this theory is correct, the number of African or African-derived slave names at Mount Vernon actually rises to about 40 percent of the total. Slave children at Mount Vernon, both male and female, were often named for relatives, a fact that reinforces the belief that their families chose their names.[28] This naming pattern also underscores the importance placed on family ties within the slave community itself.[29]

Until they joined the plantation workforce, slave children seem to have led a fairly unstructured existence. In 1799, almost three-quarters of these children lived in households headed by single parents who were almost invariably female. With their mothers away from home for most, if not all, of the dawn-to-dusk workday, the children seem to have been largely unsupervised, except by one another, or occasionally an elderly person, during those hours.[30]

We do know that the young children spent a great deal of time playing together. Washington made it a practice to forbid the children at the Mansion House Farm from coming into the yards and gardens near his house, complaining that they "too frequently are breaking limbs or twigs from or doing other injury to my shrubs." Despite the president's wishes, the children got into these off-limits areas anyway and Washington wanted his manager to break them of this practice. There is no record of the specific games that threatened Washington's carefully thought-out plantings, but the possibilities include climbing and swinging on trees, dueling with branches, riding stick horses, and a group game called "hiding the switch," in which one child hid a stick on his person and the child who found it ran after the others and tried to hit them.[31]

Other whites besides George Washington had problems with the behavior of enslaved children. One farm manager was offered use of the servants' hall, the outbuilding just to the north of the Mansion, during his first winter on the job, so that he would be better situated to learn about various aspects of his new position. He informed Washington, however, that "I had Rather Live in the house you intended for me as I have Several small Children and I should Like to keep them at a distance from the Black ones and I thought I saw a great many at your Mansion House."[32] Although this statement certainly reflects prejudice, it also suggests differing cultural attitudes between the Anglo- and African-American communities about children's behavior.[33]

Slave children too young to join the workforce appear to have done small jobs about the plantation, both for the overseers and for their own families. With most parents working long hours away from home, there must have been a multitude of small tasks the children could perform. Hauling water and wood and caring for younger children are both mentioned in surviving plantation documents. George Washington once cautioned his overseers against using any able-bodied adult slave for their own purposes. He told the men that he did not care, however, if they used one of the slave children "for the purpose of fetching wood or water, tending a child, or such like things." As soon as the child was of an age to begin fieldwork, though, Washington expected "to reap the benefit of their labour

This line engraving entitled View of Mount Vernon, The Seat of George Washington Esq. *was published by S. Scott in Edinburgh around 1796.*

myself."[34] Later that year, when he asked his farm manager to try to break the children of coming into the yard, George Washington reminded him that "they have no business within; having their wood, Water, &ct at their own doors," indicating that they had regular responsibilities for those chores within their families.[35] Slave parents may also have expected their children to do such things as weed a family garden plot, feed chickens or other fowl, or take care of mending, but we have no way of knowing for sure. Children may have done cooking occasionally as well; however, the source in this case is unclear and culinary endeavors might have been restricted to young adolescents.[36]

This period of relative freedom ended when the children were between 11 and 14 years old and became part of a transitional group to assist on the farms, called "working boys and girls." Jobs done by these older children included working on a road; cleaning brick; baking bread; carrying water to the wash house; working in the barn; hauling rails; carrying shocks of wheat and rye during the harvest; making fences; hauling manure, corn, and wheat; helping to carry oats; driving a harrow, roller, and cart; cutting down and picking corn stalks; cleaning up after the women grubbing a field; threshing wheat; daubing a house; and getting wood.[37]

RECREATION AND PRIVATE ENTERPRISE; PERSONAL TIME, PERSONAL ENTERPRISE

During their time off from work, the enslaved population at Mount Vernon found many ways to fill their "free" hours. Each evening, on Sunday, and on their occasional holidays, the slaves would have been busy with activities to benefit themselves and their families, rather than their master. Most important on a daily basis would have been "housekeeping" chores, such as tending chickens and garden plots, cooking and preserving the produce of those gardens, and caring for clothing and other aspects of personal appearance.[38]

For at least some of the slaves at Mount Vernon, personal time may have been taken up with learning to read or in teaching others. While it may not have been common, it was neither unusual nor illegal for Virginia slaves at this period to be literate. In fact, 18th-century pastors engaged in ministering to slaves often saw it as part of their duty to teach their congregants to read so that they would have access to the scriptures for themselves. It has been estimated that perhaps as many as 15-20 percent of adult slaves were literate at this period.[39]

Those slaves who worked as overseers on George Washington's farms were probably expected to read and write so that reports of work done under their supervision could be drawn up each week and orders from Washington read. For example, when Will, the overseer at Muddy Hole Farm, was sick for two weeks in February 1786, the overall reports contained no information from him, noting that there had been "no acc[oun]t given in."[40] A note dropped at the time of an escape attempt in 1799 suggests that Christopher, a young house servant, could probably read and write as well. Because he worked closely with George Washington, a certain degree of literacy may have been expected or might have been picked up as part of Christopher's job.[41]

Not only overseers and house servants could read, however. When Caesar, a field worker on one of the outlying farms, ran away in the 1790s, Washington commented that he had a good chance of

Slaves were creative in finding ways to make money. Six pence were given to a slave named Easter in exchange for a broom that had presumably been made in quarters. The handmade brooms above were featured at a recent Craft Fair at Mount Vernon

success, "as he can read, if not write."[42] It is highly unlikely that Caesar would have needed to read as part of his job, so he must have learned in some other way, possibly, given his role as a minister in the black community, through a church connection. It is clear, though, that not all the Mount Vernon slaves, not even all the house servants, were literate. Many years after she ran away, Martha Washington's former maid, Oney Judge, noted that the Washingtons had never given her any "mental . . . instruction," in all the time she was with them. She went on to relate proudly that one of her first acts upon gaining her freedom was to learn to read.[43]

A number of their "off-duty" activities would help a slave family earn money, which could then be used, however slightly, to raise their standard of living. The ways to spend this money would have been as varied as the individual people themselves; but there are indications that better clothing, extra food, and household goods were among the possibilities. When the Washingtons' cook Hercules went with them to Philadelphia during the presidency, he was able to make a good deal of money by selling "slops" from the kitchen. He was described at this period as wearing white linen, black silk breeches and waistcoat, highly-polished shoes with large buckles, a blue cloth coat with velvet collar and bright metal buttons, a watch fob and chain, cocked hat, and gold-headed cane, items much finer than the clothing issued to him.[44] Other individuals spent their money on food, usually in the form of supplies that were better than their usual rations. Fine flour, large quantities of pork, and whiskey were all purchased from George Washington by Mount Vernon slaves.[45] It is also likely that they bought imported foods, such as tea, coffee, molasses, and sugar, from shops in Alexandria. The only detailed description of the interior of a slave dwelling at Mount Vernon sketches a scene of dire poverty, brightened by the presence of "some cups and a teapot," which could well have been purchased by the family living in the cabin.[46]

Simply being alert could bring financial rewards. For example, Mount Vernon's farm manager placed a notice in a local paper about a pocketbook that had been found along the road outside of Alexandria. The rightful owner could reclaim his property after paying for the advertisement and "allowing something for the Negro who found it."[47] Special jobs might also result in a tip for a slave's services. When a slave who belonged to James Cleveland returned a horse to Mount Vernon, he was given three shillings, which he could presumably spend as he wished. Several slaves assisted George Washington in getting his valet, Billy Lee, to the home of a friend after Billy broke his knee pan while surveying with Washington; they were given six shillings in gratitude for their aid. Washington's contemporaries, benefiting from the help of his slaves, would quite likely have tipped them.[48]

George Washington often purchased foodstuffs, both from his own slaves and from those on neighboring farms as well. Eggs, chickens, ducks, melons, cucumbers, and honey all found their way from the quarters to the Mansion table over the years, and one visitor to Mount Vernon recorded that Washington's slaves also sold their chickens in Alexandria.[49] Other slaves made small items for sale. Six pence, for example, were given to a slave named Easter in exchange for a broom that had presumably been made in the quarters.[50] While some of these things may have been sold "door-to-door" in the neighborhood, another destination was the Sunday market in Alexandria, where slaves from the surrounding countryside could sell until 9:00 in the morning. This would of course have meant another very early morning for anyone trying to get into the city, which was approximately nine miles away, a 1½ to two-hour trip on horseback. The financial and social rewards, however, must have made the effort worthwhile. More than just a way to make money, the Sunday market would have been a good place to meet and develop relationships with other African Americans, both free and slave, not only from the city of Alexandria, but also from outlying plantations. Descriptions of the market in the 19th century speak of the "busy scene," probably similar to that in the previous century, as slaves squatted in the shade of trees "with their baskets of berries, their chickens and eggs."[51] Enslaved individuals from Mount Vernon needed a special pass to do business at the market in order to comply with a Virginia law that forbid sales to or purchases from slaves without the permission of their owner or overseer.[52]

Fishing and hunting were other "leisure pursuits" that could lead to financial improvement. Washington's fondness for fish was well known even outside his household, so he was a likely customer for someone with an impressive fish to sell, as when he paid three shillings for two rockfish that had been caught by "a Negroe of Capt. Marshals."[53] There is both physical and documentary evidence for the practice of hunting by the Mount Vernon slaves, which is discussed elsewhere in this book.[54] Contrary to popular belief, slaves could legally own guns under certain circumstances. Virginia law forbid them to keep firearms unless they were either traveling with their master or had written permission from him or their employer to have a gun. Washington clearly knew about and sanctioned the keeping of guns by at least some of his slaves.[55] He even provided shot on occasion, most likely for provisioning his own table or for hunting vermin.[56]

It is clear that the enslaved population at Mount Vernon was hunting not only to supplement their own diet but also to earn money. One fall, for example, two slaves, Tom Davis and Sambo, sold their master a total of 11 dozen birds; both of these men were well-known hunters.[57] Davis, who regularly supplied the Mount Vernon household with fresh game, had a "great Newfoundland dog" as his hunting companion. According to Martha Washington's grandson, ducks were extremely plentiful along the Potomac in the 18th century and one shot from Davis's old British musket generally brought down "as many of those delicious birds as would supply the larder for a week."[58] The African-born Sambo, who later took the surname Anderson, had been brought to Virginia in the 1750s, where he was trained as a carpenter. He was a rather colorful character, with gold rings in his ears and a face adorned with both ethnic scarification ("country marks") and tattoos. After Washington's death in 1799, Sambo supported himself by hunting wild game, which he sold to hotels and "the most respectable families" in Alexandria. He earned enough money from this endeavor to purchase and emancipate two slaves, both of whom were members of his family.[59] There is no reason to suppose that Sambo was not occasionally earning money from those same sources while Washington was still alive.

An interesting incident in the fall of 1787 also suggests that the Mount Vernon slaves could earn a little extra money by preventing others from hunting on Washington's property. In keeping with long-standing traditions that limited hunting on an estate to the landowner or those to whom he had given permission, Washington forbid hunting by outsiders and ordered his slaves to immediately investigate any gunshots heard on his land.[60] A "Party of young Gentlemen" sailed down from Alexandria to hunt ducks along the Potomac and had the misfortune to land their craft at Washington's River Farm. Three slaves belonging to the plantation, one of whom carried a gun, approached the young men and "insisted" that one of them shoot a squirrel, which he did. They enticed two of the group further into the woods with the promise of more squirrels, and then turned on them "in the most Violent manner" and took away their guns. As they ran off to turn the confiscated weapons over to Washington, the slaves were heard to say that they had just earned £10, probably as a reward for disarming the trespassing hunters.[61]

While it may strike people today as particularly gruesome, a perfectly acceptable means of making money was the selling of teeth to dentists. Since at least the end of the Middle Ages, very poor

Washington's Gristmill, located on Dogue Run Farm, approximately 2½ miles from the Mansion, was one of the area's most sophisticated and profitable.

people had often sold their teeth for use in both dentures and in tooth transplant operations for those wealthy enough to afford these procedures.[62] A French dentist named Jean Pierre Le Moyer or Le Mayeur emigrated to America in 1780 and treated patients between New York and Richmond over the next decade. Specializing in tooth transplants, he found that transplantable teeth were hard to come by and went so far as to advertise in the newspapers for "persons disposed to sell their front teeth, or any of them."[63] The Frenchman first treated George Washington in 1783. The following year, Washington paid several unnamed "Negroes," presumably Mount Vernon slaves, 122 shillings for nine teeth, slightly less than one third the going rate advertised in the papers, "on acct. of the French Dentis."[64] Whether the teeth provided by the Mount Vernon slaves were simply being sold to the dentist for any patient who needed them or were intended for George Washington is unknown at this point, although the fact that Washington paid for the teeth suggests that they were for his own use.[65]

Concern with his slaves' private lives came to the fore when Washington's interests were threatened by their entrepreneurial activities. In the fall of 1794, for example, he learned that Sally Green, the abandoned wife of one of his white carpenters and the daughter of his old servant, Thomas Bishop, was thinking of moving to Alexandria to open a shop. Washington feared that, given her long-standing ties to the Mount Vernon slaves, the shop would be "no more than a receptacle for stolen produce" from his farms. He asked his manager to caution Sally against dealing with his slaves, for if "she deals with them at all she will be unable to distinguish between stolen, or not stolen things." He warned that if she came under any suspicion of dealing in stolen goods, "she need expect no further countenance or support from me."[66]

The dogs kept by enslaved workers on the plantation for hunting and companionship were also an economic threat to George Washington. These animals were apparently quite well trained, for Washington commented that "it is astonishing to see the command under which their dogs are." He believed the dogs were being used during "night robberies" to round up Mount Vernon sheep, which were then sold to outside "receivers." Washington eventually ordered that, after deciding which dogs to keep on each farm, the manager should kill all the others. Then "if any negro presumes under any pretence whatsoever, to preserve, or bring one into the family . . . he shall be severely punished, and the dog hanged."[67]

In addition to their efforts to make money, the slaves at Mount Vernon also spent their free time having fun. One favorite activity seems to have been visiting with one another. Washington once noted that "it is no uncommon thing for them to be running from one house to another in cold windy nights with sparks of fire flying, and dropping as they go along."[68] He complained more than once about the slaves being too exhausted, after what he called "night walking," to do the work expected of them.[69] There is also evidence that children had the opportunity to make extended visits on other farms, presumably to relatives.[70]

During these visits, the enslaved population engaged in a number of activities. A Jew's harp found in the remains of the blacksmith shop could have been used by either a slave or a white servant and would have required no special training to play. The cellar of an excavated slave quarter on the Mansion House Farm yielded large numbers of clay pipe fragments used by both sexes for smoking tobacco.[71] As people relaxed to the sound of music or as the aroma of pipe tobacco filled the quarters, some individuals started telling stories. A number of the plantation's slaves came originally from Africa; and Martha Washington's grandson later remembered hearing stories from one of these people, an elderly man named Jack, who told the little boy tales of that far-off and exotic place and stories of his own capture and enslavement.[72] If Jack was telling such stories to the master's grandson, he and others were almost surely relating similar tales to the children of their own families. In doing so, they would have been passing on cultural values, building pride, and giving the children a historical framework for their lives. All of these things would help to fashion a community within the quarters, where the first generation of inhabitants had originally come from Africa and widely differing locales within Virginia itself.[73]

The slaves at Mount Vernon also found time for games and

sports in their free hours. Among the objects recovered from the site of a two-story quarter for slave families at Mount Vernon were clay marbles, which were the most popular game of small black boys in the 18th and 19th centuries. It is possible that this game of skill and perhaps gambling continued after childhood.[74] The Potomac River and the many creeks on the plantation provided opportunities for swimming or wading as a respite from the oppressive heat and humidity of the Virginia summer.[75] A Polish visitor once described what may have been a team sport played by the Mount Vernon slaves on their Sunday off. A group of about 30 slaves, presumably adults, were divided into two groups to play a game identified as "prisoner's base," which involved "jumps and gambols as if they had rested all week."[76] Prisoner's base was an English game dating back to the Middle Ages, which is depicted in contemporary prints and was the subject of at least one song. It was played outdoors by both children and adults of all classes in the 18th century and appears to have been a very athletic, team version of the modern game known as "Tag."[77]

George Washington occasionally let the slaves leave his home or plantation to attend special events. In the fall of 1786, for example, he permitted them to go into Alexandria to attend the horse races. Washington stipulated that, so long as responsible individuals remained on each of his farms, the others were free to stagger their attendance over the several day event.[78] Those slaves who accompanied the Washingtons to New York and Philadelphia during the presidency were given several opportunities to enjoy the entertainments available in those cities. In May 1791, Martha Washington gave two of the men tickets to a play. Two years later, her maids were given a dollar to "see the tumbling feats" and the same amount of money to "go to the Circus." They must have liked what they saw there because, within a month, two of the men were given money for the same purpose.[79]

The slaves at Mount Vernon were also included, at least occasionally, in the events surrounding milestones in the Washington family. One of the most important of these family events in the last years of George Washington's life was the marriage of his wife's youngest granddaughter, Nelly, to his nephew, Lawrence Lewis. The wedding took place on the evening of February 22, 1799, which happened to be George Washington's final birthday. In addition to various members of the extended family, there were a sizable number of slaves in attendance. About 60 years after the nuptials an elderly bondswoman described the wedding to the bride's great-niece. She recalled that Mrs. Washington had "let all the servants come in to see" the wedding and also provided them with "such good things to eat" on the day of the wedding, indicating that they also partook of some of the party delicacies.[80] While it is doubtful that all of the slaves from the outlying farms would or even could have been invited to the festivities, it is conceivable that the approximately 90 slaves physically close to the Washingtons on the Mansion House Farm, some of whom were very likely emotionally close, were included. Less than a year after Nelly's wedding, an even more significant event transpired, which would ultimately have a great effect on the personal lives of the slaves at Mount Vernon. On December 14, 1799, George Washington died after a short illness and was buried in the family vault, following Anglican and Masonic funeral rites four days later. Two young slaves, Cyrus and Wilson, actually took part in the ceremonies, leading Washington's horse, which was carrying his saddle, holster, and pistols, in the funeral procession from the Mansion to the tomb. After the services, the hundreds of guests who

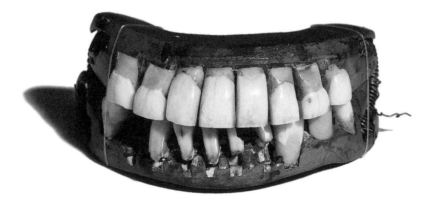

In 1787, Washington paid several unnamed "Negroes," presumably Mount Vernon slaves, 122 shillings for nine teeth. It is unknown whether these teeth were used in making Washington's own dentures, or resold to a dentist for a profit.

took part in the funeral were offered something to eat and drink. When they were gone, the "remains of the provisions" were distributed to the slaves.[81]

Very little is known at present about the spiritual life of the Mount Vernon slaves. There is no evidence that George and Martha Washington took any interest in the religious beliefs of their slaves, something few plantation owners did in the 18th century.[82] In fact, one of the major complaints of Oney Judge, Mrs. Washington's former maid, who converted to Christianity in the years after she ran away, was that she "never received the least . . . moral instruction, of any kind, while she remained in Washington's family."[83] There are indications that the slave community at Mount Vernon may have developed spiritual leaders of its own. On the 1799 slave list, Will at Muddy Hole Farm has the letters "Mintr" written beside his name. It has been suggested that he was a "minister," something that would not have been unknown in Virginia at this period.[84] Another slave, Caesar, at Union Farm, was said to have been a well-known preacher among the local black population in the last years of the 18th century. He was described as often wearing clothing that was black and white in color, perhaps a way of indicating his ministerial role.[85]

A description left by an 18th-century visitor suggests the Mount Vernon slaves were in contact with Baptists, Methodists, and Quakers. Prince Louis-Philippe of France and his servant talked with a number of the slaves and recorded that these three religious groups had raised the hopes of slaves at Mount Vernon that they would receive their freedom in the not too distant future. The Quakers had even approached the Mount Vernon slaves at places described as "clubs," possibly meetings of mutual aid or self-help societies, in Alexandria and Georgetown.[86] Throughout Virginia in the last half of the 18th century, Baptists and Methodists actively sought new members from the slave community and, whether through their open acceptance of them into the congregation as equals or their anti-slavery message, were met with an enthusiastic response, especially from those who were younger and had been born in America. The presence of Baptists and Methodists among the Mount Vernon slaves is therefore something to be expected.[87]

There are also several tantalizing hints that religious traditions from Africa, or at least their influence, had not completely died out at Mount Vernon by the end of the 18th century. Apparently this was not unusual; evidence of similar cultural survivals has been found at Monticello in Virginia, in Maryland, and in South Carolina. African-born slaves generally continued to practice their native religions after their enslavement and transportation to the Americas, with these traditions surviving the longest in areas where the population had a high concentration of Africans.[88] Archaeologists working in the cellar of a Mount Vernon slave quarter found a raccoon baculum or penis bone that had been incised along one end, transforming it into a ceremonial or decorative object that may well have been worn suspended from a cord around someone's neck. They also found the leg bone of an owl, bearing knife marks where the talons had been cut off, again probably so that they could be worn. These objects, treated in greater detail elsewhere in this book, certainly suggest the practice of other belief systems besides, or perhaps in conjunction with, Christianity on George Washington's estate and lend credence to an undocumented tradition that the slaves at Washington's Dogue Run Farm, at least, practiced voodoo or conjuring.[89] There is also some evidence that elements of Muslim culture, if not the actual practice of that religion, continued at Mount Vernon up to the very early 19th century.[90]

LAST THINGS

For those slaves who did not outlive George Washington, freedom came only through death. At the end of their lives, they were laid to rest in one of several cemeteries scattered throughout the plantation. The cemetery at the Mansion House Farm is located in a quiet, wooded area near the Washington family tomb. Grave markers present in the 19th century have disappeared over the years, but remote sensing of this site revealed the presence of about 50 graves, oriented on an east-west axis. While this is the customary western model for burials, there is a tradition in the local African-American community that the bodies were laid this way so that they faced Africa, symbolizing their desire to return home.[91] Before being lowered into the grave, the bodies were first placed into coffins made by the plantation's carpenters.[92] There is also evidence for some sort of social gathering associated with the death. In 1787, Hercules, the cook at Mount Vernon for many years, was given three bottles of rum at the request of Martha Washington in order "to bury his wife." The rum was probably shared with other mourners, either at a wake or at a meal after the funeral, although it may have been used as payment to people who washed the body and otherwise prepared it for burial.[93]

In summary, while the African Americans who lived and worked at Mount Vernon seem to have been fairly typical of slaves on large plantations throughout Virginia, they probably had more freedom over certain aspects of their lives than the average modern visitor would suspect. In both its childrearing and marriage practices, the Mount Vernon slave community appears to have differed from the dominant white society and to have lived by its own norms. Individuals were given time and permission to travel locally in order to form and sustain their family relationships. In their time off from work, the Mount Vernon slaves engaged in tasks that would earn them small sums of money to better their lives. They also enjoyed time with their friends, took part in local cultural events, and nurtured their spiritual lives. While all of this may not sound too different from the way people live today, we must never forget, as the slaves could not, that at any time their master could change his mind about allowing a certain liberty. When that happened, there might be no more trips to a social club in Alexandria, a valuable and beloved pet might die, or a marriage, like Fanny's, no matter how difficult, might be abruptly ended without the consent of the two people most concerned.

NOTES

1. Washington to Burwell Bassett, 5/23/1785, *The Writings of George Washington from the Original Manuscript Sources, 1745-1799*, ed. John C. Fitzpatrick 39 vols. (Washington, D.C., 1931-1944), 28:152.

2. William Waller Hening, *The Statutes at Large; Being a Collection of All the Laws of Virginia, From the First Session of the Legislature, in the Year 1619*, 13 vols. (Richmond, Va., 1823), 12:182. See also a similar law of October 1748 in ibid., 6:109.

3. Washington to Roger West, September 9, 1799, *Writings*, 37:367-368.

4. Washington to John Francis Mercer, November 24, 1786, *Writings*, 29:83. For similar sentiments, see also Washington to Lund Washington, February 24-26, 1799, and Washington to John Fowler, February 2, 1788, *Writings*, 14:148, 29:398.

5. Washington to David Stuart, February 7, 1796, *Writings*, 34:452-453.

6. Lund Washington to Washington, February 18, 1778, March 4, 1778, *Lund Washington Papers*, Mount Vernon Ladies' Association, Mount Vernon, Virginia (typescript). For a similar case, see Lund Washington to George Washington, December 3 and 17, 1775, and Lund Washington to George Washington, January 17,1776, January 25,1776, and February 8, 1776, W. W. Abbott et al., eds., *The Papers of George Washington*, 45 vols. to date (Charlottesville, Va., 1976-), *Revolutionary War Series*, 2:478, 570, and 3:126, 188.

7. Lund Washington to George Washington, March 11, 1778, *Lund Washington Papers*.

8. Weekly Report, February 21, 1795, *Washington Papers*, Library of Congress (photostat, PS-140, Mount Vernon Ladies' Association).

9. Washington to William Pearce, March 1, 1795, *Writings*, 34:128. For other examples of a master intervening in a slave marriage, see Gerald W. Mullin, *Flight and Rebellion: Slave Resistance in Eighteenth-Century Virginia* (New York, 1972), 28 and 65; Elizabeth Fox-Genovese, *Within the Plantation Household: Black and White Women of the Old South* (Chapel Hill, N.C., and London, 1988), 299.

10. On the subject of early African-American marriage, see Herbert G. Gutman, *The Black Family in Slavery and Freedom, 1750-1925* (New York, 1977), 87-93, 131. The gender ratio on Washington's individual farms may have affected marriages there. Of the five farms which made up the Mount Vernon estate, only the Mansion House Farm was home to more men than women; the population on the other four farms was overwhelmingly female. Many people, in other words, would have been forced to look off the farm on which they lived, in order to find a mate.

11. Mount Vernon slave list, February 18, 1786, in *The Papers of George Washington: The Diaries of George Washington*, 4:277-283 (hereafter referred to as 1786 Slave List); "NEGROES belonging to George Washington in his own right and by Marriage," [June 1799], and "A List of Negroes Hired from Mrs. French," July 15, 1799, *Writings*, 37:256-268, 308-309 (hereafter referred to collectively as 1799 Slave List).

12. Washington to Hector Ross, October 9, 1769, *Writings*, 2:526.

13. Washington to Anthony Whiting, May 19, 1793, *Writings*, 32:465. For an example of how common inter-plantation visiting was in the 18th century, see Richard Parkinson, *A Tour in America in 1798, 1799, and 1800* (London, 1805), 448. For the importance of Sundays and holidays to slave children, see David K.

Wiggins, "The Play of Slave Children in the Plantation Communities of the Old South, 1820-60," *Growing Up in America: Children in Historical Perspective*, ed. N. Ray Hiner and Joseph M. Hawes (Urbana, Ill., and Chicago, 1985), 182-183.

14. Louis-Philippe, *Diary of My Travels in America*, trans. Stephen Becker (New York, 1977), 31-32.

15. Weekly Reports, February [16] and March 23, 1793, Thom Collection, A-283, Mount Vernon Ladies' Association.

16. Sandy Newton, Research notes on midwives and childbirth at Mount Vernon, May 31, 1992 (typescript, Mount Vernon Ladies' Association), 2-3.

17. Washington to William Pearce, August 17, 1794, *Writings*, 33:469. Lund Washington, February 20, 1775, and April 28, 1783, Lund Washington Account Book, 1774-1786, Mount Vernon Ladies' Association (typescript, Mount Vernon Ladies' Association), 51, 121 (hereafter referred to as Lund Washington Account Book); Mount Vernon Farm Ledger, July 25, 1796, Washington Papers, Library of Congress (photostat, PS-140, Mount Vernon Ladies' Association), 75.

18. Washington, December 4, 1786, *Diaries*, 5:75. See also William Pearce to Washington, August 31, 1794, Washington Papers, Library of Congress (typescript, PS-10, Mount Vernon Ladies' Association). For information on maternal death rates during childbirth at this period, see Laurel Thatcher Ulrich, *A Midwife's Tale: The Life of Martha Ballard, Based on Her Diary, 1785-1812* (New York, 1992), 170-173.

19. *Mount Vernon Store Book*, December 1-31, 1787 (typescript, Mount Vernon Ladies' Association) (hereafter referred to as Mount Vernon Store Book). For the use of rum as a restorative after childbirth, see Ulrich, A Midwife's Tale, 190.

20. Weekly Reports, February [16], 1793, Thom Collection.

21. Weekly Reports for the spring of 1798, in Mount Vernon Farm Accounts, September 16, 1797-March 24, 1798 and March 31, 1798-January 1799, Archives of the Morristown National Historical Park, Morristown, N.J. (photostat, Mount Vernon Ladies' Association).

22. Karin Calvert, informal talk on the history of childhood, 1600-1830, Mount Vernon, July 2, 1991; Christy Coleman Matthews, then Director of the Department of African-American Interpretation at Colonial Williamsburg, conversation with the author, July 22, 1995; *Before Freedom Came: African-American Life in the Antebellum South*, ed. Edward D.C. Campbell and Kym S. Rice (Richmond, Va., and Charlottesville, Va., 1991), 109; Constance B. Schulz, "Children and Childhood in the Eighteenth Century," *American Childhood: A Research Guide and Historical Handbook*, ed. Joseph M. Hawes and N. Ray Hiner (Westport, Conn., and London, 1985), 79.

23. George Washington to George Augustine Washington, September 2, 1787, *Writings*, 29:269.

24. Washington to William Pearce, November 29, 1795, *Writings*, 34:379.

25. Lund Washington Account Book, September 6, 1783 (typescript), 125. For

examples of special care given to new mothers and the material goods used as incentives for women to produce and successfully raise children on other plantations, see Gutman, *The Black Family*, 76-77.

26. Gutman, *The Black Family*, 194-195; Marvin L. Michael Kay and Lorin Lee Cary, *Slavery in North Carolina, 1748-1775* (Chapel Hill, N.C., and London, 1995), 138-139.

27. For similarly imposed names, see Kay and Cary, *Slavery in North Carolina*, 139-149, 268-277, and Peter H. Wood, *Black Majority: Negroes in Colonial South Carolina from 1670 through the Stono Rebellion* (New York, 1974), 181-186, 181n.

28. See the 1786 and 1799 Slave Lists.

29. The slaves at Mount Vernon were not unique in these naming patterns. Historians studying slaves on other plantations have found evidence that children were often named after parents or other relatives (see Kay and Cary, *Slavery in North Carolina*, 163; Gutman, The Black Family, 186-199).

30. Only at River Farm in 1795 does there appear to have been someone assigned to watch over the children. See Weekly Reports, February 14 and 21, May 30, December 5, 12, and 19, 1795, Washington Papers, Library of Congress (photostat, PS-140, Mount Vernon Ladies' Association). Having older children look after younger ones may well have been the norm in the plantation south. For instance, slave children at Monticello who were under the age of ten were expected to "serve as nurses," presumably for the younger children. See Elizabeth Dowling Taylor, "The Plantation Community Tour" (unpublished paper prepared for the interpreters at Monticello, February 1993 and revised March 1994), 2. See also Schulz, "Children and Childhood in the Eighteenth Century," 79; Bernard Mergen, Play and Playthings: A Reference Guide (Westport, Conn., and London, 1982), 39; Daniel Blake Smith, "Autonomy and Affection: Parents and Children in Eighteenth-Century Chesapeake Families," Growing Up in America: Children in Historical Perspective, ed. N. Ray Hiner and Joseph M. Hawes (Urbana, Ill., and Chicago, Ill., 1985, 45-58), 55; Wiggins, "The Play of Slave Children," 175, 187.

31. Washington to William Pearce, October 27 and December 22, 1793, Writings, 33:142-143, 201. See also George Augustine Washington to Washington, December 14, 1790, in The Papers of George Washington: Presidential Series, 7:80-81. For evidence that George Washington found the presence of small, noisy children of all races "disagreeable," see Anthony Whiting to Washington, January 16, 1793, manuscript, A-301, Mount Vernon Ladies' Association (typescript, Mount Vernon Ladies' Association). For games played by slave children, see Wiggins, "The Play of Slave Children," 178-179, 180, 182; Mergen, *Play and Playthings*, 41, 43, 51-52.

32. Washington to William Pearce, October 6, 1793, *Writings*, 33:111; William Pearce to Washington, October 19, 1793, *Washington Papers*, Library of Congress (typescript, PS-10, Mount Vernon Ladies' Association). Washington's efforts to control where the children played were mirrored by a few later slave owners. Interviews conducted in the 1930s with former slaves from throughout the

south indicate that at least 10 percent of their former masters made similar attempts to restrict where and when the children could play.

33. Similar concerns about conflicting values and their effect on Anglo-American children were expressed by other 18th-century writers. See Parkinson, *A Tour in America*, 435-436; Mechal Sobel, *The World They Made Together: Black and White Values in Eighteenth-Century Virginia* (Princeton, N.J., 1987), 64-67, 135-139.

34. Washington to the overseers at Mount Vernon, 7/14/1793, *Writings*, 33:11.

35. Washington to William Pearce, October 27, 1793, *Writings*, 33:142-143. See also Washington to Anthony Whiting, November 25, 1792, and Washington to James Anderson, November 1, 1798, *Writings*, 32:240, 37:2.

36. George Augustine Washington to George Washington, August 20, 1790, in *The Papers of George Washington: Presidential Series*, 6:312. For evidence that these chores were fairly typical for slave children, see Wiggins, "The Play of Slave Children," 175.

37. 1799 Slave List; Washington, July 15, 1786, *Diaries*, 5:8-10; Weekly Reports, February 24, 1787, March 3, , 17, 24, and 31, 1787, April 7, 14, and 21, 1787, manuscript, W-1174, Mount Vernon Ladies' Association (typescript, Mount Vernon Ladies' Association). The fact that slave children at Mount Vernon started working at the ages of 11 to 14 should not be seen as anything unusual for the period. Depending on their sex, slave children at Monticello began working at the age of ten, in either the nailery or as spinners, and spent the next six years at those jobs, until they were able to start fieldwork or entered a trade. See Taylor, "The Plantation Community Tour," 2. Interviews with freed slaves from throughout the south, recorded in the 1930s, suggest that a similar pattern was followed on other plantations (see, Wiggins, "The Play of Slave Children," 175).

38. Looking after and arranging hair seems to have been an important aspect of African culture that continued in African-American society in the 18th century. For more on this topic, see Shane White and Graham White, "Slave Hair & African American Culture in the Eighteenth and Nineteenth Centuries," *The Journal of Southern History* 61 (February 1995), 45-76.

39. Mullin, *Flight and Rebellion*, 76, 80-81, 93-94, 111, 114, 121, 130, and 190n.; Sobel, *The World They Made Together*, 184-185; Peter Kolchin, *American Slavery, 1619-1877* (New York, 1993), 141-142. For estimates on the percentage of slaves who were literate in the 18th century, see Robert William Fogel, *Without Consent or Contract: The Rise and Fall of American Slavery* (New York and London, 1989), 156-157. Laws prohibiting the public teaching of reading and writing to groups of slaves were passed in Virginia in the 19th century, but were largely ignored; see Kolchin, *American Slavery*, 129, and Calder Loth, ed., *Virginia Landmarks of Black History: Sites on the Virginia Landmarks Register and the National Register of Historic Places* (Charlottesville, Va., 1995), 41. For discussions of education among slaves, see Eugene D. Genovese, *Roll, Jordan, Roll: The World The Slaves Made* (New York, 1974), 561-6, and Janet Duitsman Cornelius, *When I Can Read My Title Clear: Literacy, Slavery, and Religion in the Antebellum South*

(Columbia, S.C., 1991).

40. Weekly Reports, February 11 and 25, 1786, *Washington Papers*, Library of Congress (photostat, PS-17, Mount Vernon Ladies' Association).

41. Washington to Roger West, September 19, 1799, *Writings*, 37:367-368. Another intriguing possibility is that Will, who was Christopher's uncle, may have taught his nephew this important skill. Given the connection between religion and literacy in the slave community at this period, it is also interesting to note that Will may have been a minister. Thus, he might have taught Christopher to read not only out of family responsibility but out of his religious beliefs, as well.

42. Washington to William Pearce, February 21, 1796, *Writings*, 34:476.

43. Benjamin Chase, "Mrs. [?] Staines," *Slave Testimony: Two Centuries of Letters, Speeches, Interviews, and Autobiographies*, ed. John W. Blassingame (Baton Rouge, La., 1977), 249.

44. George Washington Parke Custis, *Recollections & Private Memoirs of Washington* (Philadelphia, 1861), 423.

45. Mount Vernon Farm Ledger, 1797-1798, Archives of the Morristown National Historical Park (photostat, Mount Vernon Ladies' Association), 168, 191.

46. Julian Niemcewicz, *Under Their Vine and Fig Tree: Travels Through America in 1797-1799, 1805*, ed. Metchie J.H. Budka, (Elizabeth, N.J., 1965), 100.

47. *Alexandria (Virginia) Gazette*, October 27, 1798.

48. Lund Washington Account Book, August 18, 1783, April 22, 1785, 125, 149.

49. Mary V. Thompson, "Better . . . Fed Than Negroes Generally Are?": Diet of the Mount Vernon Slaves" (Mount Vernon Ladies' Association, June 1993), 15-16; Niemcewizc, Under Their Vine and Fig Tree, 101.

50. Ledger B, September 13, 1792, *Washington Papers*, Library of Congress (photostat, Mount Vernon Ladies' Association), 344a.

51. T. Michael Miller, ed., *Pen Portraits of Alexandria, Virginia, 1739-1900* (Bowie, Md., 1987), 281-282; Mary G. Powel, *The History of Old Alexandria, Virginia From July 13, 1749 to May 24, 1861* (Richmond, Va., 1928), 58-59.

52. *Columbian Mirror and Alexandria (Virginia) Gazette*, June 12, 1798; Hening, Statutes, 12:183.

53. Ledger B, September 11, 1790, 320a.

54. For more on this topic, see Dennis Pogue's essay in this volume. Dennis J. Pogue and Esther C. White, "Summary Report on the "House for Families" Slave Quarter Site (44 Fx 762/40-47), Mount Vernon Plantation, Mount Vernon, Virginia" (Mount Vernon Ladies' Association, December 1991), 33; Stephen C. Atkins, "Mount Vernon Identified Taxa" (Mount Vernon Ladies' Association, 1993). For hunting on other plantations, see Parkinson, A Tour in America, 446; and Lucia Stanton, "'Those Who Labor for My Happiness': Thomas Jefferson and His Slaves," Jeffersonian Legacies, ed. Peter S. Onuf (Charlottesville, Va., 1993), 166.

55. Hening, Statutes, 12:182.

56. Mount Vernon Store Book, January 19, 1787.

57. Ledger B, October 2, 1792, 346a.

58. Custis, Recollections, 457-458.

59. Dorothy S. Provine, ed., Alexandria County, Virginia Free Negro Registers, 1797-1861 (Bowie, Md., 1990), 105, 209; M. to Mr. Snowden, "Communicated," *Alexandria (Virginia) Gazette*, November 16, 1835; "Mount Vernon Reminiscences," *Alexandria (Virginia) Gazette*, January 18, 22, and 25, 1876.

60. *Alexandria (Virginia) Gazette*, August 10, 1786; Washington to Archibald Johnston, October 30, 1787, Writings, 29:295-296.

61. Joseph Lewis, Jr., to Washington, November 12, 1787, *The Papers of George Washington: Confederation Series*, 5:431-432.

62. Elisabeth Bennion, *Antique Dental Instruments* (New York and London, 1986), 82; Bernhard Wolf Weinberger, *An Introduction to the History of Dentistry*, 2 vols. (St. Louis, Mo., 1948), 1:357, 366.

63. Washington, Diaries, 4:193n-194n; *The Papers of George Washington: Confederation Series*, 3:337n-338n; Weinberger, History of Dentistry, 1:355, 366.

64. Lund Washington Account Book, May 1784, 134.

65. See Washington to Richard Varick, February 22, 1784, Writings, 27:342-343, for evidence that Washington was changing his mind about the efficacy of the transplantation process and thus might have undergone the procedure sometime later.

66. Washington to William Pearce, 11/16/1794, 11/30/1794, *Writings*, 34:24-25, 48.

67. Washington to Anthony Whiting, 11/18/1792, 12/16/1792, *Writings*, 32:232, 264. Washington was not the only plantation owner to resort to such measures. Thomas Jefferson, on at least one occasion, ordered the destruction of all dogs belonging to his slaves, while permitting his overseer to retain a couple for his own use. At least one of those dogs was hung. Barbara McEwan, *Thomas Jefferson: Farmer* (Jefferson, N.C., and London, 1991), 128; Zanne McDonald, Research Department, Thomas Jefferson Memorial Foundation, Monticello, Virginia, conversation with the author, October 5, 1993. For other references to slaves using dogs for hunting and efforts to control the same, see Landon Carter, *The Diary of Colonel Landon Carter of Sabine Hall, 1752-1778*, ed. Jack P. Greene, 2 vols. (Charlottesville, Va., 1965), 1:72-73, 75, 77, 86, 87, 254, 258, 261, 299, 335; Custis, *Recollections*, 66; Hening, *The Statutes at Large*, 6: 295-296; Parkinson, *A Tour in America*, 446. For further information on slaves and dogs, see John Campbell, "My Constant Companion: Slaves and Their Dogs in the Antebellum South," *Working Toward Freedom: Slave Society and Domestic Economy in the American South*, ed. Larry E. Hudson, Jr. (Rochester, N.Y., 1994), 53-76.

68. Washington to William Pearce, February 9, 1794, *Writings*, 33:267.

69. Washington to William Pearce, May 18, 1794, *Writings*, 33:369; Washington to James Anderson, February 20, 1797, Thom Collection, A-301.201, Mount Vernon Ladies' Association.

70. 1786 Slave List, 280.

71. Pogue and White, "Summary Report," 24-27.

72. Custis, Recollections, 456.

73. Music and storytelling were pastimes the Mount Vernon slaves had in common with slaves on other plantations. Members of the Jefferson household and their slaves shared a lively musical tradition, and, very much like young "Washy" Custis, Thomas Jefferson's daughter Martha grew up listening to tales related by slaves (see Stanton, "Those Who Labor for My Happiness," 166-67). For storytelling to children on later 19th-century plantations, see Wiggins, "The Play of Slave Children," 182.

74. Pogue & White, "Summary Report," 33. Bernard Mergen, "Top-time's Gone, Kite-time's Come, and April Fool's Day Will Soon Be Here: Making Time for Play in the Early Republic" (paper presented at a seminar on "Pleasant Diversions: Americans at Leisure, 1750-1875," George Mason University, March 19, 1993); Mergen, Play and Playthings, 8, 11, 41, 42, 45; Wiggins, "The Play of Slave Children," 180.

75. Lund Washington to George Washington, 9/2/1778, Lund Washington Papers (typescript).

76. Niemcewicz, Under Their Vine and Fig Tree, 101.

77. Jane Carson, Colonial Virginians at Play (Williamsburg, Va., 1989), 44; Merilyn Simonds Mohr, The Games Treasury (Shelburne, Vt., 1993), 310-311; Iona and Peter Opie, Children's Games in Street and Playground (London, 1969), 7, 9-10, 143-146; Mergen, Play and Playthings, 8, 74.

78. Washington, Diaries, 5:49, 50.

79. Stephen Decatur, Jr., Private Affairs of George Washington (Boston, 1933), 233. [Tobias Lear and Bartholomew Dandridge], April 1, 1793, June 24, 1793, July 13, 1793, "Washington's Household Account Book, 1793-1797," parts 1-8, The Pennsylvania Magazine of History and Biography 29, no. 4 (1905), 385-406; 30, no. 1-4 (1906), 30-56, 159-186, 309-331, 459-478; 31, no. 1-3 (1907), 53-82, 176-194, 320-350.

80. Agnes Lee, Growing Up in the 1850s, ed. Mary Custis Lee deButts (Chapel Hill, N.C., and London, 1984), 80-81.

81. Tobias Lear, Letters and Recollections of George Washington (New York, 1906), 138-141.

82. The custom of having simple household services became more common in the 19th century and was practiced by Mrs. Washington's grandson's family at Arlington, where at least the domestic slaves were typically included, and more formal church services were even held for the slaves in a little schoolhouse on Sundays. Kolchin, American Slavery, 54, 55, and Murray H. Nelligan, Old Arlington: The Story of the Lee Mansion National Memorial (Washington, D.C., 1953), 118. See also Augusta Blanche Berard to Mrs. Mary Berard, April 18, 1856, in "Arlington and Mount Vernon, 1856," introduction and notes by Clayton Torrence, Virginia Magazine of History and Biography (April 1949), 161, and "Mount Vernon As It Is," Harper's New Monthly Magazine (March 1859), 445.

83. Chase, "Mrs. [?] Staines," Slave Testimony, 249.

84. Charles C. Wall, "Housing and Family Life of the Mount Vernon Negro" (Mount Vernon Ladies' Association, May 1962), 25-26; Morgan, "Slave Life in Piedmont Virginia," *Colonial Chesapeake Society*, ed. Lois Green Carr, Philip D. Morgan, and Jean B. Russo (Chapel Hill, N.C., 1988), 479.

85. Philip D. Morgan and Michael L. Nicholls, "Slave Flight: Mount Vernon, Virginia, and the Wider Atlantic World" (Mount Vernon Ladies' Association, 1995), 12.

86. Louis-Philippe, *Diary of My Travels*, 32. See Stanton, "Those Who Labor for My Happiness," 168, for a discussion of the religious life of the slaves at Monticello.

87. Kolchin, *American Slavery*, 55-57; Morgan, "Slave Life in Piedmont, Virginia," 472-79; Sobel, *The World They Made Together*, 187-98.

88. Stanton, "Those Who Labor for My Happiness," 168; Kolchin, *American Slavery*, 54-55.

89. Pogue and White, "Summary Report," 44-46; Paul Leland Haworth, *George Washington: Country Gentleman* (Indianapolis, Ind., 1925), 213.

90. For a fuller treatment of religious beliefs among the Mount Vernon slaves, and especially the possible practice of Islam and other belief systems outside Christianity, see Mary V. Thompson, "And Procure for Themselves a Few Amenities": The Private Life of George Washington's Slaves," *Virginia Cavalcade* (Autumn 1999), 187-91 and Thompson, "Religious Practice in the Slave Quarters of Mount Vernon," *Colonial Williamsburg Interpreter* (Spring 2000), 10-14.

91. Dennis J. Pogue, Director of Restoration at Mount Vernon, conversation with the author, February 7, 1995; "The Slave Memorial at Mount Vernon" (brochure from the 11th anniversary of the slave memorial, Mount Vernon Ladies' Association, Mount Vernon, Virginia, September 17, 1994), 1.

92. Weekly Report, April 7, 1787, *Washington Papers*, Library of Congress (photostat, PS-17, Mount Vernon Ladies' Association).

93. Storehouse Account Book, September 9, 1787; Leni Ashmore Sorensen, consultant on African-American history and graduate student at the College of William and Mary, conversation with the author, November 4, 1994.

Archaeologists dig slowly and carefully to uncover artifacts at the site of the House for Families.

Slave Lifeways at Mount Vernon: An Archaeological Perspective

Dennis J. Pogue

A s was generally the case at large agricultural enterprises throughout the American South during the 18th century, the labor of enslaved Africans was the engine driving the complex, multi-functioning system that was George Washington's Mount Vernon plantation. Archaeological excavations at the site of the "House for Families," the main slave dwelling located at the Washingtons' "Mansion House Farm," have yielded a rich assemblage of domestic artifacts and food remains associated with the house servants and craftspeople that lived there. By analyzing the material record of this under-documented group, it has been possible to add to the developing picture of daily life that this segment of the Mount Vernon slave community experienced. This essay will relate those insights, as well as illustrate the challenges inherent in interpreting the archaeological record of slavery in 18th-century America.

Archaeology and Slavery at Mount Vernon

The House for Families was a large frame building that up until 1793 served as the main slave quarter at the Mount Vernon home farm. Its location on the north lane of outbuildings, situated directly across from the blacksmith's shop, is depicted on a plan of the estate drawn by Samuel Vaughan, an admirer of General Washington's, after he visited Mount Vernon in 1787. There is no record of its construction during George Washington's ownership of Mount Vernon. Therefore, it is possible that Lawrence, George Washington's older brother, erected this quarter after acquiring the plantation in 1743 from their father, Augustine. Lawrence owned the plantation until his death in 1752. This quarter housed the majority of the slaves living at the Mansion House Farm, one of five farms that together comprised the approximately 8000-acre Mount Vernon plantation.[1]

A painting attributed to Edward Savage (ca. 1792) is the only surviving contemporary depiction of the House for Families. In the painting, it appears to be a substantial building, two stories in height, at least six bays in length, and with chimneys in each gable. That it was frame is indicated by a reference to reusing the "old plank ripped off the old Quarter" for weather board on a "Necessary" being built to accommodate the inhabitants of the "New Quarter." Virtually no other evidence pertaining to the earlier quarter is available.[2]

The House for Families was demolished in the winter of 1792-93, when the slaves moved into new quarters located in one-story wings attached to either side of the nearby greenhouse. Archaeological excavations revealed the remnant of a small (six-foot-square), brick-lined cellar located within the conjectured limits of the footprint of the structure. Using the location of the cellar as a starting point, it is possible to estimate the size of the building. The cellar is oriented square with the quarter as it is depicted in the Savage view. Measuring from the far wall of the cellar to the east gable wall of the reconstructed new quarter indicates that the old quarter was at least 55 feet in length. Once again, by measuring from a line extending from the corner of the new quarter to a point that incorporates the cellar within the building, the width would be at least 35 feet. At 1,925 square feet per floor, the building would have had almost 4,000 gross square feet of space.[3]

While these dimensions make it an unusually large slave quarter, at least by the standards of mid-18th-century Virginia, it is unlikely that all of the 67 slaves known to have been in residence at the Mansion House Farm in 1786 could have lived in this space. Other apparently smaller cabins are known to have been located nearby, as a visitor in 1795 noted that "the cabins for the slaves" were arranged in a group situated north of the Mansion in the general vicinity of the new quarter. While this visitor was observing the conditions as they existed a few years after the House for Families had been replaced by the new quarter, it seems likely that additional slave cabins to complement the main quarter were a long-term necessity.[4]

The 67 slaves living at the Mansion House Farm performed a wide variety of duties that supported the Washington household as well as the broader activities of the entire plantation. These duties included serving not only as house servants, but also as blacksmiths, carpenters, masons, coopers, gardeners, and spinners and weavers. Most of the remaining slaves were field hands working under the direction of overseers at the four outlying farms.[5]

Once it ceased to be used in its original storage function, the cellar served as a handy trash receptacle, and it has yielded an extremely rich assemblage of domestic refuse. The household items recovered include a wide variety of ceramics, table glass, table utensils, wine bottles, tools, and personal items such as tobacco pipes, buttons and buckles, and the like. The cellar was filled with refuse over a span of many years and was finally capped with structural debris when the building was demolished. At a preliminary level of analysis, little in this assemblage provides even a hint that those who discarded the objects were African-American slaves rather than a relatively prosperous planter family (Table 1).[6]

One unusual and suggestive artifact was recovered that represents Mount Vernon's best candidate for an object reflecting an African cultural tradition. This is the baculum (penis bone) of a raccoon, which has been modified by incising a line encircling one end. Only a few raccoon elements are included among the 25,000 bones recovered from the cellar. The bone therefore seems to have served a special function, possibly as some sort of ceremonial device or decorative item. Raccoon bacula are relatively large (from 93 to 111 millimeters) and distinctively curved, and the male raccoon is known to be sexually aggressive. The combination of these characteristics suggests its selection as a fertility symbol suspended around the neck. Such a practice need not be viewed as particularly African, however, as similarly modified bacula have been excavated from numerous prehistoric Native American sites; and therefore it seems more likely to reflect a pancultural folk practice.[7]

The generally high quality of the domestic materials provides additional evidence that slaves living near the planter's household benefited from that proximity by receiving items second hand. Obviously, this alone does not mean that their daily life was any less onerous. The slaves living at the Mansion House Farm were generally

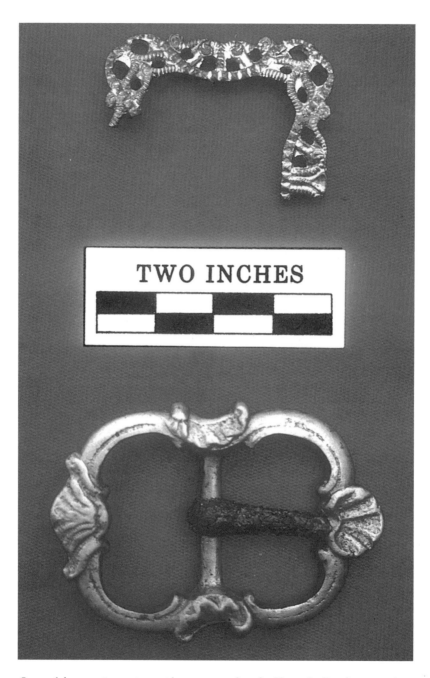

TWO INCHES

Some of the more interesting artifacts uncovered at the House for Families are a shoe buckle (top) and a strap buckle.

more skilled and performed more valued tasks than did the field hands, however, and as a result may well have enjoyed higher status. Such appears to have been the case in the South generally, and abundant documentary evidence supports that interpretation at Mount Vernon.[8]

Perhaps the best example of preferential treatment by the Washingtons toward an individual slave is that of the cook, Hercules. While serving the presidential household in Philadelphia, he was allowed to sell leftover foodstuffs, from which he realized a profit of up to $200 annually. With this income, he was able to purchase such items as fine clothes, a cane, a watch, and ornate shoe buckles. Ironically, in 1797, while still in Philadelphia, Hercules ran away rather than return with the family to Mount Vernon as planned at the end of the president's second term. Neither Hercules nor his family, at least one daughter of whom remained behind in servitude, apparently had any second thoughts about his decision, even though the cook arguably occupied the highest status of any of the Washingtons' slaves, being held in high regard by both his fellow slaves and his master. This circumstance is a reminder that too much significance may be given to relatively comfortable material conditions. Hercules was, after all, a slave, and the fact that he wore fine shoe buckles and expensive clothing did nothing to change that fact.[9]

Other items recovered from the cellar seem to reflect the occupation of many of the slaves who lived at the quarter, namely domestic servitude in the Washington household. In particular, the many buttons (30) and shoe buckles (11) suggest the type of apparel worn by the male slaves who served in the Mansion. Of the 30 buttons, 18 are in sizes typically associated with men's coats and waistcoats. The shoe buckles include two that have a relatively intricate molded decoration, one of which still retains portions of a decorative silver wash. Other clothing items include two shirt studs, at least one pair of cufflinks, five glass discs that might be cufflink inserts, and two copper alloy watch fobs. Whether or not any of these objects were purchased specifically for the use of the slaves is difficult to ascertain. Washington did order buttons specifically to outfit his house servants, and several of the white metal buttons recovered fit the description of some of the buttons purchased for their use. Finally, theft may explain the presence of some objects in the cellar, especially the small decorative items like the watch fobs and cufflinks.[10]

Glass beads, another category of artifact found in significant numbers (49), also are related to personal adornment. Seven of the beads (14.2 percent) are blue in color and the preference for blue beads has been hypothesized as an African cultural survival. Blue beads seem to have been used widely in Africa, and they have been recovered in some quantities from American sites associated with slaves. This association requires further testing, however, as beads are commonly found at 18th-century Anglo-American sites as well; and the color blue is ubiquitous. For example, of a sample of 366 glass beads deriving from five Potomac River sites spanning the period from 1638 to 1730, 78 percent are either blue or blue with white stripes.[11]

The detailed analysis of patterns within the ceramic assemblage supports the inference that the tablewares at least were passed down from the Washingtons to the slaves when those items had fallen out of fashion. The most common ceramic type recovered is English white salt-glazed stoneware, popular both in England and America from the 1720s until the late 1760s (Table 2). The earliest documented occasion of George Washington's ordering stoneware for use at Mount Vernon dates to 1757. Its popularity declined rapidly with the introduction in 1762 of a new tableware, Josiah Wedgwood's creamware. As an example of George Washington's desire to keep current with the newest fashion trends, in July 1769 he was one of the first in America to order a full setting (250 pieces) of the new ware. The shipment reached Virginia a year later and creamware appears to have quickly replaced white salt-glazed stoneware on the Washingtons' table.[12]

While both white salt-glazed stoneware and creamware were recovered from the cellar, the stoneware accounts for 28 percent of the ceramic fragments found, while creamware makes up only 8 percent. Moreover, the stoneware represents numerous vessels (25) and a variety of vessel types — tea cups and saucers, mugs, small bowls, and chamber pots in addition to plates. This volume and diversity suggests that the Washingtons passed the stoneware down to the quarter as a set, instead of individually as damaged pieces.

The detailed studies of ceramics and food remains have been particularly rewarding modes of analysis. Patterns in the types of ceramic vessels used by slaves, and in the diversity and the quality of slave diet, were first identified by several pioneering studies in the 1970s and were hypothesized as indicative of the relatively impoverished economic condition and the dependent status inherent in slavery. Over the intervening years, considerable additional evidence has been found to indicate that slaves used a relatively higher proportion of bowls than planter households, from which they apparently ate one-pot meals. Other evidence for the prevalence of such meals was provided by the presence of finely chopped animal bones, which also reflected generally poor cuts of meat. Another finding is that, in general, the diet of slaves was much more diverse than the stereotypical reliance on rations of pork and corn meal,

A selection of the varied artifacts discovered at the House for Families cellar excavation.

This detail from the 1792 painting of Mount Vernon attributed to Edward Savage shows the House for Families, which was located quite close to the Mansion.

supplemented by small amounts of vegetables grown in gardens.[13]

A total of 58 different animal species are represented in the House for Families collection of more than 25,000 faunal elements. George Washington operated a fishery on the nearby Potomac River as a commercial venture and, according to his writings, he also used a major portion of the annual catch as rations for his slaves. This is borne out by the archaeological record, as a large percentage (28.3 percent) of the bones recovered from the cellar fill are freshwater fish: primarily catfish, bass, and perch. The evidence from the cellar also indicates that Washington's slaves were able to augment their rations of fish, cornmeal, beef, and pork by hunting wild game, by fishing, and by raising chickens. In addition to cow and pig bones, which are easily the most numerous domestic species represented, bones of wild fowl such as quail, duck, goose, and turkey; and wild animals such as deer, squirrel, rabbit, and opossum, as well as non-schooling fish such as pickerel, gar, and bluegill, have been recovered. Bones of young chickens and egg shells also were found (Table 3).[14]

On the other hand, while a remarkable diversity of animal types are represented, it is clear that the Mount Vernon slaves still depended on only a few species for the great majority of their food. These findings are consistent with dietary patterns found in virtually every faunal assemblage associated with slaves studied to date, indicating that beef and pork were the main meat sources. At Mount Vernon, beef provided 37.4 percent of the diet, with pork second at 24.6 percent, and fish third at 16.8 percent. Mutton (8.7 percent) and a large number of species of wild fowl (6.7 percent) and wild mammals (4.2 percent) added variety to the menu.[15]

While beef and pork have been identified as the two most important sources of meat in slave diets, the proportion of beef in the Mount Vernon assemblage is unusually high. This high percentage may reflect the elevated status enjoyed by the slaves living in the House for Families. On the other hand, it may be a characteristic of the diet for all of the slaves on the plantation, and thus could be a reflection of the relative affluence of George Washington and an idiosyncrasy of his provisioning system rather than a result of any special treatment of his servants and craftsmen. Unfortunately, until a comparable sample of faunal data associated with an outlying quarter becomes available for study, it is not possible to address this issue further.[16]

Two interrelated questions raised by the presence of large numbers of bones from wild species pertain to the manner by which the slaves obtained the non-rationed food, and whether this activity was sanctioned by Washington and other planters. Gun parts have been found at many sites elsewhere that were occupied by slaves, and numerous lead shot and gun flints were recovered from the Mount Vernon cellar. This pattern is so widespread that there seems little doubt that the slaves were using the firearms themselves in hunting. That slaves sometimes hunted game for their master's table at Mount Vernon is well documented, but the number of bones from wild species found suggests that slaves in general had much more ready access to guns than has been believed. Obviously, some of the animals could have been trapped as well. The non-schooling fish may have been caught using hook and line.[17]

One of the rare contemporary accounts that refers to slave life at Mount Vernon is that of Julian Niemcewicz, a Polish visitor to the plantation in 1798: "A very small garden planted with vegetables was close by (the quarter), with 5 or 6 hens, each one leading ten to fifteen chickens. It is the only comfort that is permitted them [the slaves]; for they may not keep either ducks, geese, or pigs. They sell the poultry in Alexandria and procure for themselves a few amenities." There is no doubt that Niemcewicz was describing a quarter located at one of the outlying farms instead of at the Mansion House Farm, but his account supports the interpretation that slaves were able to supplement their rations and, more surprisingly, their income.[18]

As a result of the intensive analysis of the bone fragments, it also is possible to determine the size and age of the animal and the cut of meat. This information allows identification of the types of meals that were prepared, as well as provides some sense of the quality of the meat. As with other studies, numerous small fragments were recovered. Abundant evidence for what are traditionally identified as poor meat cuts — feet and heads and other less fleshy portions — also was found. But bones reflecting meatier, high quality cuts also were recovered in only slightly lower percentages. Thus, the Mount Vernon data suggest that the pattern of poor cuts of meat is too simplistic, and the recent findings from other African-American sites in the region and elsewhere seem to correlate with the evidence from the House for Families. On the other hand, the more desirable species of fish, such as sturgeon and smallmouth and largemouth bass, were not found; and the fish that were recovered generally are small, weighing less than one pound.[19]

The prevalence of one-pot meals, with meat and vegetables cooked together, also has been identified as a strong West African cooking tradition, which the archaeological data suggest continued in America. One needs to be careful before characterizing this as an ethnic marker, however, as a functional cause also seems plausible. The preparation of stews is a likely tactic when confronted with meats of uneven quality and stews were also a staple of Anglo-American cuisine throughout this same period.[20]

Excavation of the cellar of the House for Families reveals that pork served as approximately 25 percent of a slave's meat diet on the Mansion House Farm.

One artifact type that has been found to correlate to a degree with sites occupied by slaves is colonoware. This is a locally made, hand-built, low-fired and unglazed ceramic that has been recovered from 18th-century contexts in large quantities in South Carolina and in significant, if considerably fewer, numbers in Virginia. For many years it was assumed that this pottery was made by local Native Americans and either sold or traded to planters, or directly to slaves, for their use. Recent scholarship suggests that in South Carolina African Americans made much of the colonoware, and there seems to be no doubt that at least some of the colonoware in Virginia was made by slaves and/or free blacks.[21]

The contrast between the European-made fine tablewares and the coarse, locally-made colonowares in the Mount Vernon assemblage is striking and begs explanation. The overwhelming majority — eight of the 11 vessels that are identifiable as to form — of the colonoware fragments are from the same vessel type, small undecorated bowls that seem more likely to have served in the consumption of food rather than in its preparation (Table 2). As the faunal and documentary evidence point to stews and other pottages as a common type of meal eaten by slaves, perhaps the presence of the colonoware bowls is related to the practice of eating such dishes from small individual bowls. Bowls made of the imported wares also appear in significant numbers in the cellar ceramic assemblage, with bowls making up 26.4 percent of all vessels. The presence of the colonoware bowls in addition to the bowls that had been handed down therefore may reflect the unusual importance placed on this type of vessel in this context.

As for the layout and use of the interiors of the slave quarters at Mount Vernon, unfortunately no descriptions of either the House for Families or the later quarter that replaced it are known to exist. But the size and floorplan of the second quarter, built of brick and consisting of four rooms each 35 x 20 feet in size, with one doorway serving each room, point to a communal living situation. Additional partitioning of the spaces to allow a measure of privacy for family units also could well have occurred. Based on the only surviving graphic depiction of the House for Families quarter — the painting from 1792 — it also appears to have been a substantial building, at least two stories in height, and built of wood on a brick foundation. That between 40 and 50 slaves may have resided in this structure points to its also having been a communal residence, with several families and other people likely living together in each of the four to eight rooms such a structure could have accommodated.[22]

In contrast, the quarters located at the other, outlying farms seem to have been much smaller log "cabins," many of which are known to have been built by the slaves themselves. These structures were so insubstantial, in fact, that when George Washington embarked upon a general reorganization of the layout of the slave dwellings in the 1790s, several of the cabins were simply picked up and moved.[23]

The account by Niemcewicz mentioned above provides a remarkably graphic depiction of the domestic scene he observed at one of these outlying farms, which further suggests that the Mansion House Farm slaves may have been living more comfortably than their fellows: "We entered one of the cabins of the Blacks, for one can not call them by the name of houses. They are more miserable than the most miserable of the cottages of our peasants. The husband and wife sleep on a mean pallet, the children on the ground; a very bad fireplace, some utensils for cooking, but in the middle of this poverty some cups and a teapot." The reference to the tea wares is particularly interesting given the archaeological evidence of such ceramics recovered from the cellar.[24]

Niemcewicz was understandably appalled by his exposure to the American slave system, remarking that "General Washington treats his slaves far more humanely than do his fellow citizens of Virginia. Most of these gentlemen give to their Blacks only bread, water and blows." The latter observation undoubtedly was an overstatement; but, based on documentary evidence, the treatment of slaves by their masters varied considerably from plantation to plantation depending on the economic position, the personal beliefs, and the idiosyncrasies of masters. The location and size of the plantation, the crops being grown and the labor system used, and the number of slaves in residence were also important factors affecting slaves' treatment. Thus, important variation among domestic assemblages associated

123

The excavation of the cellar of George Washington's House for Families was made much more difficult by the presence of modern intrusions such as water pipes.

with slaves should be anticipated when slave quarters from the similarly varied contexts known to exist in the Colonial Chesapeake are excavated.[25]

"MOUNT VERNON AND BEYOND"

Based on this new evidence, our evolving picture of slave life at Mount Vernon suggests a less controlled existence than does the stereotypical view of slavery. The diet of the slaves living in the House for Families certainly was more diverse, and therefore probably was more healthful, than previously was believed. That the slaves were able to hunt, fish, raise poultry, and garden to supplement their food allotment, may in turn imply some free time and more choice as to how they could spend that time. On the other hand, what appears more likely is that the slaves felt the need to augment their rations because of limitations in them that they perceived. At any rate, the greater diversity of slave diet and the ability of the slaves to raise, hunt, and gather additional food is a pattern that archaeologists have discovered at numerous other plantations throughout the South.[26]

Combining the archaeological findings with the documentary evidence also suggests that the practice of slavery at George Washington's plantation fits well with the overall picture of slavery in the Chesapeake that has emerged over the last decade. According to recent syntheses of the history of slavery in America, by the late 18th century the Chesapeake had emerged as a true slave society, with both a native-born master class and slave population. Although the Mount Vernon plantation was unusual in the region because of its relatively large size and correspondingly populous slave community, Washington's paternalistic attitude, the demographic stability of the slave population, and the strong familial and community ties that appear to have been forged as a result of the steady growth of the population by natural means, all seem characteristic of slavery in Virginia and Maryland.[27]

Given this profile, scholars have argued that by the end of the century, a new African-American culture was developing that saw the slow erosion of specific African cultural traits. Crucial to this development was the fact that the proportion of African-born slaves

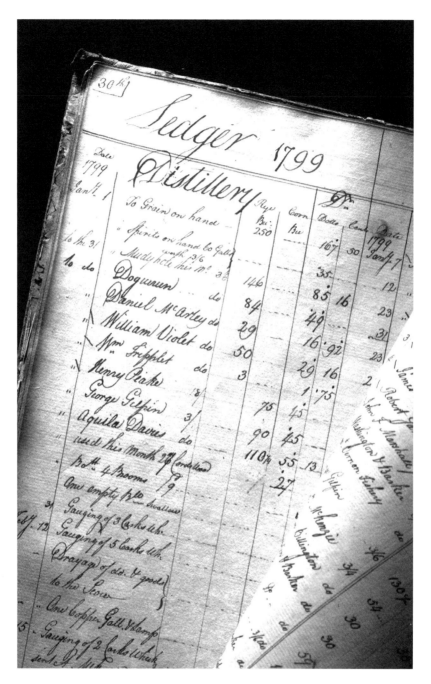

The ledger from George Washington's distillery reflects a busy and profitable business. Archaeology is currently being conducted at the original distillery's site.

in the region declined precipitously throughout the century, making up only one-tenth of the population as early as the 1770s. As a consequence of this trend, the virtual absence of obviously African or African inspired objects recovered archaeologically no longer is surprising.[28]

One interpretation of the results of the recent research suggests that by the time of the American Revolution, white and black Virginians had developed a culture that was a merger of European and African traditions, that both blacks and whites held a mix of quasi-English and quasi-African values. Although clearly there is much evidence to support the view that the emerging American culture was fundamentally the product of the interaction of English, African, and Native American traditions, the assessment that "this thesis of cultural homogenization takes a legitimate point too far" seems appropriate. While heavily influenced by each other, it seems more likely that "black Southerners built a distinctive African-American culture based on their shared experiences under slavery and white Southerners built their own distinctive society based on their shared experiences with slavery." Thus, we should expect to find subtle but significant differences between Chesapeake slaves and slaves from other regions where conditions differed. This does in fact appear to be the interpretive pattern that is slowly evolving.[29]

One instructive comparative exercise is the contrast between the demographic characteristics and the archaeological records of 18th-century Virginia and South Carolina. Unlike in Virginia, the African population in South Carolina was in the majority as early as the 1720s and exceeded 60 percent for most of the century. In addition, the preponderance of slaves was concentrated in the low country parishes and was commonly divided into holdings numbering in the hundreds. In Virginia, the proportion of the total population made up by slaves was much smaller, only 30 percent by 1720 and less than 40 percent in 1790, and the slaves were typically distributed in groupings of less than 50 individuals. Thus, the demographic conditions in South Carolina seem to have been much more conducive to retaining African traditions than seems to have been the case in Virginia. Since contact with whites was much more pervasive in Virginia, creolization at a relatively accelerated rate was more likely.[30]

Archaeologically, the differences between the two colonies are best illustrated thus far by comparing the colonoware found in Virginia with that from South Carolina. Distinct contrasts in the characteristics of the colonowares from the two colonies have been attributed to the fundamentally different demographic conditions. First of all, colonoware is found throughout the state and in much greater quantities in South Carolina, which indicates that the ware was in much wider use there. Second, South Carolina colonoware appears to have retained a much closer affinity to its presumed African precursors. This is evidenced by a greater variety of vessel forms and marked similarities between them and African vessels. Finally, based on the presence of apparent ritual symbols incised into the pots themselves, colonoware in the low country seems to have been vested with symbolic and ritualistic meanings that appear to be absent in Virginia.[31]

As significant as the archaeological evidence retrieved from the cellar at the House for Families may be in interpreting the lifeways of the slaves who lived there, the fact remains that this evidence represents a minority of the bound inhabitants of Mount Vernon. More than two-thirds of Mount Vernon slaves lived in the dispersed quarters located at the four outlying farms. Moreover, the slaves at the home farm were overwhelmingly employed as house servants and craftsmen, in contrast with the field hands who lived at Dogue Run, Muddy Hole, Union, and River Farms. Until a similar sample of material culture associated with the field hands is excavated and analyzed, the picture of domestic life at Mount Vernon will remain incomplete. Unfortunately, so far the sites of those quarters have proven elusive, largely because of the highly developed character of the Mount Vernon neighborhood and the resulting disturbance of the sites by residential construction.[32]

Evidence for the daily lives of slaves in Virginia as a whole is similarly limited. To date, scarcely more than a score of slave domestic sites from 18th-century Virginia have been excavated, and the majority of those are home quarters associated with large plantations. The material culture associated with slaves living in what were the most common conditions of the period — at small to middling farms and plantations where fewer than five slaves worked alongside the planter family — remains almost completely unexamined. Further, as at Mount Vernon, even at the large plantations where home quarters have been studied, few if any outlying quarters have been excavated to provide a source of direct comparison.

Thus, the findings of the last two decades of archaeological research on the African presence in the American South must still be viewed as highly tentative. The variability of those results should no longer come as a surprise, however, given the important differences in the day-to-day experience among the slaves at Mount Vernon, in the Chesapeake, and in America as a whole. In this respect, the traditional dependence on ethnicity as an organizing device has been found to have significant limitations. Rather than taking into account the fluctuating character of interpersonal relations both within the African-American community and between blacks and whites. such a focus emphasizes the identification of distinct normative behaviors. Instead a reconceptualization of the interaction of the two groups as a highly dynamic process seems to offer much greater promise for a better understanding of those relationships.[33]

TABLE 1

ARTIFACTS RECOVERED FROM THE
HOUSE FOR FAMILIES CELLAR

ARTIFACT TYPE	NUMBER	
Ceramics	578	(fragments)
Bottle glass	521	(fragments)
Table glass	66	(fragments)
Tobacco pipe	561	(fragments)
Pewter spoon	4	
Bone handled table knife	4	
Buttons (pewter/bone/copper)	30	
Shoe buckles (copper/iron)	11	
Strapping buckles	17	
Glass beads	49	
Shirt studs	2	
Cufflinks	1	pair
Glass cufflink inserts	5	
Watch fob	2	
Bone fan blade	1	
Straight pins	244	
Iron needle	1	
Furniture tack	10	
Clock spring	1	
Bone brush ferrule	1	
Pot hook	1	
Pot	1	
Clay marble	4	
Socket chisel	1	
Draw knife	1	
File	1	
Shovel	1	
Broad hoe	1	
Gun flint	2	
Lead shot	124	
Window glass	167	(fragments)
Door lock	1	
Horse shoe	2	
Harness boss	1	
Harness eyelets	3	
TOTAL	**2420**	

TABLE 2

CERAMICS FROM THE
HOUSE FOR FAMILIES CELLAR

WARE	SHERDS		VESSELS		BOWLS	
	No.	%	No.	%	No.	%
Colonoware	38	6.5	13	9.5	8	61.5
Misc. coarse earthenwares	47	8.1	13	9.5	4	30.7
Slipware	103	17.8	18	13.3	0	0
Tin-glazed earthenware	73	12.6	15	11.0	8	53.3
Misc. refined earthenwares	27	4.6	8	5.8	1	12.5
Creamware	37	6.4	9	6.6	1	11.1
Pearlware	9	1.5	3	2.2	1	33.3
White salt-glazed stoneware	154	26.6	25	18.3	4	16.0
Brown salt-glazed stoneware	10	1.7	7	5.1	0	0
Rhenish stoneware	17	2.9	6	6.6	2	33.3
Chinese porcelain	63	10.8	19	13.9	7	36.8
TOTAL	578	100.0	136	100.0	36	26.4

TABLE 3

FAUNAL REMAINS FROM THE
HOUSE FOR FAMILIES CELLAR

TYPE	BIOMASS	PERCENTAGE
Total domestic species	43.4	71.6
Cow	22.6	37.4
Pig	14.9	24.6
Sheep	5.3	8.7
Bird	0.6	1.0
Total wild species	17.1	28.3
Fish	10.1	16.8
Bird	4.0	6.7
Mammal	2.6	4.2
Miscellaneous	0.4	0.6
TOTAL	**60.5**	**100.0**

NOTES

1. The earliest known reference to this structure may be George Washington's note in 1761, that "lightning struck My Quarter and near 10 Negroes in it," Donald Jackson and Dorothy Twohig, eds., *The Diaries of George Washington*, 6 vols. (Charlottesville, 1976-79), 1:281; W. W. Abbott, et al., eds., *The Papers of George Washington*, 45 vols. to date (Charlottesville, 1976-) *Confederation Series*, 5:432-433; *The Papers of George Washington: Colonial Series*, 1:234.

2. John C. Fitzpatrick, ed., *The Writings of George Washington from the Original Manuscript Sources, 1745-1799*, 39 vols. (Washington, D.C., 1931-44), 31:307-308.

3. Washington directed his plantation manager, Anthony Whiting, to remove the old quarter in a letter dated October 14, 1792, *Writings*, 32:182; Dennis J. Pogue and Esther C. White, "Summary Report on the 'House for Families' Slave Quarter Site (44Fx762/40-47), Mount Vernon Plantation, Mount Vernon, Virginia," *Quarterly Bulletin of the Archeological Society of Virginia* 46 (1991), 189-206.

4. As the 18th century progressed, large communal quarters like the House for Families became increasingly more unusual, Philip D. Morgan, *Slave Counterpoint: Black Culture in the Eighteenth-Century Chesapeake and Lowcountry*

(Chapel Hill, 1998), 103-110. Washington made a census of the Mount Vernon slave community in 1786, listing a total of 216 slaves on the plantation. Jackson and Twohig, *Diaries of George Washington*, 4:277-279; Isaac Weld, *Travels Through the States of North America, and the Provinces of Upper and Lower Canada, During the Years 1795, 1796, and 1797* (2nd ed., London, 1799), 92.

5. Jackson and Twohig, *Diaries of George Washington*, 4:277-284.
6. Pogue and White, "House for Families Slave Quarter," 189-206.
7. William H. Burt, *Bacula of North American Mammals* (Ann Arbor, Mich., 1960), 8; Bernhard Grzimek, ed., *Grzimek's Animal Life Encyclopedia* (New York, 1984), 12:100-101; Richard E. Steams, "The Hughes Site: An Aboriginal Village Site on the Potomac River in Montgomery County, Maryland," Proceedings of the Natural History Society of Maryland 6 (1940), 12; Robert L. Stephenson and Alice L.L. Ferguson, "The Accokeek Site: A Middle Atlantic Seaboard Culture Sequence," University of Michigan Museum of Anthropology, Anthropological Papers 20 (1963), 166.
8. John W. Blassingame, *The Slave Community: Plantation Life in the Antebellum South* (New York, 1980), 250-251.
9. George Washington Parke Custis, *Recollections and Private Memoirs of Washington* (New York, 1860), 423; Writings, 37:578; Fritz Hirschfeld, *George Washington and Slavery: A Documentary Portrayal* (Columbia, Mo., 1997), 70-71.
10. Stephen Hinks, "A Structural and Functional Analysis of Eighteenth Century Buttons" (M.A. thesis, College of William and Mary, Williamsburg, 1988), 30 and 91. George Washington ordered buttons of several types, including "white mettal buttons best kind," for use on the livery of his house servants, *Writings*, 37:443.
11. Theresa A. Singleton, "The Archaeology of Slave Life," in *Before Freedom Came: African-American Life in the Antebellum South*, ed. Edward D.C. Campbell Jr. and Kym S. Rice (Charlottesville, 1991), 164; Linda France Stine, Melanie A. Cabak, and Mark D. Groover, "Blue Beads as African American Cultural Symbols," *Historical Archaeology* 30(1996), 49-75; Henry M. Miller, Dennis J. Pogue, and Michael A. Smolek, "Beads from the Seventeenth-Century Chesapeake," Proceedings of the 1982 Glass Trade Bead Conference, ed. Charles F. Hayes (Rochester, New York, 1983), 132-138.
12. Susan G. Detweiler, *George Washington's Chinaware* (New York, 1982), 23, 53-57; Ann Smart Martin, "'Fashionable Sugar Dishes, Latest Fashion Ware': The Creamware Revolution in the Eighteenth-Century Chesapeake," in *Historical Archaeology of the Chesapeake*, ed. Paul A. Shackel and Barbara J. Little (Washington, D.C., 1994), 174-177.
13. James Deetz, *In Small Things Forgotten: The Archaeology of Early American Life* (Garden City, N.Y., 1977), 146-153; John S. Otto, "Race and Class on Antebellum Plantations," *Archaeological Perspectives on Ethnicity in America*, ed. Robert Schuyler (New York, 1980), 3-13; Dennis J. Pogue and Esther C. White, "Reanalysis of Features and Artifacts Excavated at George Washington's Birthplace, Virginia," *Archeological Society of Virginia Quarterly Bulletin* 49 (1994),

41-42; Sam B. Hilliard, "Hog Meat and Cornpone: Foodways in the Antebellum South," *Material Life in America, 1600-1860*, ed. Robert B. St. George (Boston, 1988), 311-332.

14. Joanne Bowen, "Faunal Remains from the House for Families Cellar" (Ms. on file, Mount Vernon Ladies' Association, 1993), 9-22; Stephen C. Atkins, "An Archaeological Perspective on the African-American Slave Diet at Mount Vernon's House for Families" (M.A. thesis, College of William and Mary, Williamsburg, 1994); James Wharton, "Washington's Fisheries at Mount Vernon," Commonwealth (1952), 11-13, 44.

15. Bowen, "Faunal Remains from the House for Families," 9-22; Joanne Bowen, "Faunal Remains and Urban Household Subsistence in New England," *The Art and Mystery of Historical Archaeology*, ed. Anne E. Yentsch and Mary C. Beaudry (Boca Raton, Fla., 1992), 267-281.

16. Larry W. McKee, "Plantation Food Supply in Nineteenth-Century Tidewater Virginia" (Ph.D. diss., University of California, Berkeley, 1988), 130-131; Bowen, "Faunal Remains from the House for Families," 58.

17. Singleton, "An Archaeological Framework for Slavery and Emancipation, 1740-1880," *The Recovery of Meaning: Historical Archaeology in the Eastern United States*, ed. Mark Leone and Parker B. Potter, Jr. (Washington, D.C., 1988), 349-350; Mary V. Thompson, "'They Appear to Live Comfortable Together': Private Lives of the Mount Vernon Slaves," in this volume.

18. Julian Niemcewicz, *Under Their Vine and Fig Tree: Travels in America in 1797-1799, 1805*, ed. and trans. Methcie J. E. Budka (Elizabeth, N.J., 1965), 100-101.

19. Bowen, "Faunal Remains and Urban Household Subsistence," 267-281; Bowen, "Faunal Remains from the House for Families," 9-22.

20. Stacy Gibbons Moore, "'Established and Well Cultivated': Afro-American Foodways in Early Virginia," *Virginia Cavalcade* 39 (1989), 70-83; Henry M. Miller, "Colonization and Subsistence Change on the 17th-Century Chesapeake Frontier" (Ph.D. diss., Michigan State University, Lansing, 1984).

21. Susan L. Henry, "Physical, Spatial, and Temporal Dimensions of Colono Ware in the Chesapeake, 1600-1800" (M.A. thesis, Catholic University, Washington, D.C., 1980); L. Daniel Mouer, Mary Ellen N. Hodges, Stephen R. Potter, Susan L. Henry Renaud, Ivor Noel Hume, Dennis J. Pogue, Martha W. McCartney, and Thomas E. Davidson, "Colonoware Pottery, Chesapeake Pipes, and 'Uncritical Assumptions,'" in "I, Too, Am America": *Archaeological Studies of African-American Life*, ed. Theresa A. Singleton (Charlottesville and London, 1999), 83-115; Leland Ferguson, *Uncommon Ground: Archaeology and Early African America* (Washington, D.C., 1992).

22. George McDaniel, *Hearth and Home* (Philadelphia, 1982), discusses partitioning of 19th-century slave cabins to accommodate multiple families.

23. *Writings*, 33:196.

24. Niemcewicz, *Vine and Fig Tree*, 100.

25. Niemcewicz, *Vine and Fig Tree*, 101.

26. Singleton, "Archaeology of Slave Life," 171-172.

27. Peter Kolchin, *American Slavery, 1619-1877* (New York, 1993), 28-62; Morgan, *Slave Counterpoint.*

28. Kolchin, *American Slavery*, 38.

29. Mechal Sobel, *The World They Made Together: Black and White Values in Eighteenth-Century Virginia* (Princeton, 1987), 233; Kolchin, *American Slavery*, 60-61.

30. Kolchin, *American Slavery*, 240, 46-49; Morgan, *Slave Counterpoint.*

31. Ferguson, *Uncommon Ground*, 35-39, 63, 109-116.

32. Pogue and White, "Features and Artifacts Excavated at George Washington's Birthplace," 32-45.

33. Jean E. Howson, "Social Relations and Material Culture: A Critique of the Archaeology of Plantation Slavery," *Historical Archaeology* 24 (1990), 78-91; Ferguson, *Uncommon Ground*, xli-xliii; Garrett Fesler and Maria Franklin, "The Exploration of Ethnicity and the Historical Archaeological Record," *Historical Archaeology, Identity Formation, and the Interpretation of Ethnicity*, ed. Maria Franklin and Garrett Fesler (Williamsburg, 1999), 1-10.

This photograph of an African American man named Tom was taken in the mid-19th century. One of Martha Washington's dower slaves (from her first husband's estate), Tom later became the property of her second granddaughter. This ambrotype is the only known portrait of a former Washington slave.

Beyond Mount Vernon: George Washington's Emancipated Laborers and Their Descendants

Edna Greene Medford

"Upon the decease [of] my wife, it is my Will and desire th[at] all the Slaves which I hold in [my] own right, shall receive their free[dom]."[1]

With this simple statement of intent, George Washington irrevocably altered the lives of more than 100 men and women of color, many of them having labored on his Mount Vernon estate since birth. This singular act has tempered the ordinarily harsh criticisms reserved for slaveholders and has cast Washington in a role that he may have desired, but took great care to avoid during his lifetime. Despite the significance of his actions — especially at a time when leaders of the new nation debated the moral and economic justification for slavery's continuation — comparatively little attention has been directed toward his role as slaveholder and emancipator. Hence, we know scarcely anything about the enslaved people who lived and labored at Mount Vernon and for whose manumission he provided shortly before his death. With the exception of George Washington Parke Custis's assertion that "they succeeded very badly as freemen," history has remained virtually silent on the fate of the freed people and their descendants.[2]

To a degree, the paucity of studies involving Washington's enslaved laborers reflects the unique problems inherent in reconstructing the histories of people whose lives began in bondage. The frequent absence of (or variously spelled) surnames, the contemporaneous use of certain given names, inaccurate birth dates and ages, and other examples of faulty record-keeping all confound the researcher of enslaved people at Mount Vernon, as they do anyone studying an unfree population.[3] Although there are daunting problems, extant documentary records (with the occasional assistance of oral tradition) permit a glimpse into the lives of Washington's emancipated laborers and their descendants in the generation or two beyond the granting of freedom.

In 1799, the year Washington died, 317 enslaved people lived and labored on one of the five farms that comprised his Mount Vernon estate. The former president owned 124 bondsmen and women outright. Forty other souls consisted of hired laborers, provided through a lifetime contract with Penelope French, whose more than 500 acres of land he had rented since 1786.[4] The remaining 153 belonged to the estate of Martha Washington's first husband, Daniel Parke Custis.[5] Since Custis had died intestate, Virginia law stipulated that his widow receive a life interest in one third of his property. Upon her death, his enslaved workers, known as dower slaves, passed to the Custis heirs.[6]

Over the years, the Washington and Custis laborers had intermarried. In his will, Washington expressed concern for the inevitable heartache that would result from his slaves acquiring their freedom while the dower slaves remained in bondage. In an attempt to lessen the "most painful sensations, if not disagreeable consequences" of separating the two groups, he instructed that emancipation of his slaves should occur upon his wife's death, when a general division and distribution among the heirs would be required anyway.[7] Hence, those enslaved would suffer a single disruption. Deviating from his wishes somewhat, Martha Washington chose to execute the provisions of her husband's will on January 1, 1801, a little more than one year after his death.[8] Forty men, 37 women and 47 children thus entered the ranks of the free.

In the decades that followed, some of the dower slaves acquired their freedom as well. Illustrative of this manumission is the case of Kitty Fox, who was registered as a free black woman in Alexandria County in 1831. Although the registration indicated that she had been emancipated by Martha Washington on January 1, 1801, the 1799 inventory Washington compiled within months of his death documents a single individual named Kitty, a dower slave who was wife to Isaac. The possibility that she is the same woman listed in the inventory is strengthened by the registration on the same day of 21-year-old Isaac Fox (likely her son).

Washington's list of Mount Vernon slaves clearly makes the distinction between his own slaves and dower slaves. Washington could free his slaves, but not those who were part of Martha's first husband's estate.

Similarly, when Lucinda Seaton registered as a free woman in Alexandria that same year, she too, was identified as having been "emancipated by the late General Washington."[9] Yet, the only person identified as Lucinda in the 1799 inventory — the two year old daughter of Betty — fell into the dower category of slaves.[10] An 1827 registration entry for Alexandria County listed 24-year-old Negro Lucinda who received her freedom at some unspecified time from George Washington Parke Custis.[11] The approximate ages of the two women differ by a few years, but the physical descriptions are quite similar. Perhaps the freedom of some of the dower slaves came so near that of the other Washington slaves that they (and apparently county officials as well) assumed that their emancipation was the result of Washington's will.

There was no mistaking the path by which Louisa, the two-year-old daughter of Judith, "one of the slaves in the Dower of the late Mrs. Martha Washington and lately a resident of Mt. Vernon," secured her freedom. George Washington Parke Custis, the Washington grandson, freed the child in Alexandria in 1803. Louisa likely was the daughter of unmarried 21-year-old Judy, the dower slave who labored at the Mansion House.[12]

What we know about the former bondspeople and their children we owe primarily to the registers for documenting free blacks that were established throughout the South in the first half of the 19th century. The registers for Alexandria and Fairfax counties originated with a 1793 Virginia law requiring free people of color to declare their status with the clerk of the court in the jurisdiction where they lived. The law compelled African Americans who resided in the countryside to reregister every three years and town dwellers to make declaration annually.[13]

The registers recorded the name, age, general description, and nature of emancipation of each person who claimed free status. Several dozen registrants claimed their freedom through George Washington, either directly or as the offspring of the manumitted laborers. They include the surnames Richardson and Gray, Quander and Blackburn, Jones and Jasper, among others. Those who failed to provide surnames — whether purposely or otherwise — ensured a degree of anonymity, both then and now. Moreover, it is virtually impossible to determine how many of the people registered were actually former slaves of Washington or descendants of his bondsmen and women, since not all of the registrants supplied this information. Those who had registered for the first time prior to 1822 would not have been required to give the details of their emancipation at this later period. Hence, the register often stated simply that "an original certificate of Registration" was on file.

Inconsistencies in spelling, as well, hinder a comparison of the county registers with the 1799 inventory. Thomasin (spelled variously as Thomson and Thomazin) Gray and her children, for instance, claimed free status by virtue of her manumission by Washington; but no one by that name appears in his records.[14] Instead, the inventory lists Gray under the name Formasin. Similarly, in consecutive entries of the Fairfax County register, both Matilda and Barkley Clarke are listed as children of Ginny, but the 1799 inventory records their mother as Linney. Later entries in the register correct the earlier mistake.[15]

On occasion, persons claiming emancipation were born years after Martha Washington freed her husband's slaves and thus could not have been the direct beneficiaries of the Washington will.[16] Since African Americans who claimed free status would have been required to provide incontrovertible evidence of the circumstances of their freedom, it is doubtful that any would have risked being denied certification by giving knowingly inaccurate information. Hence, it is more likely that the person making the claim to direct manumission may have been the free born offspring of a former slave who remained closely associated with the plantation.

Lapses in procedure and the infrequency of registration suggest that although the law required free people of color to register with the courts at regular intervals, authorities apparently made little or no effort to enforce it. Many of the free blacks who registered after 1822 apparently did so for the first time, including those who would have been required under law to register sooner. It is also quite possible that even in the repressive environment of antebellum Virginia, some free people of color (including the former slaves of

ZSun-nee Kimball Matema is a descendant of Caroline Branham, who worked as a housemaid for the Washingtons, and later lived and worked at Arlington House.

Washington) were able to avoid the registers altogether and thus remained anonymous (at least in certain public records).

Despite their deficiencies, the registers provide ample evidence that significant numbers of the freed blacks and their children remained in Fairfax County or ventured no farther than Alexandria. Although difficult at this juncture to determine exactly where the bulk of them settled, presumably those who shared kinship with the dower slaves maintained a physical presence close to their relatives still held in bondage. Over a dozen families had been created from intermarriages of Washington and Custis bondsmen and women, including those of the two blacksmiths, Nat and George, who had married the dower slaves Lucy and Lydia, respectively. Another such union between Sall and the dower slave Joe produced five children.[17] The emancipated spouses of those still held to labor likely found employment and lodging at Woodlawn, the estate of Eleanor Parke Custis Lewis (or Nelly, Martha Washington's granddaughter); at Arlington, the home of George Washington Parke Custis; or at the other nearby plantations and farms where hired free men and women of color routinely labored alongside the enslaved.

The separations caused by the Washington will doubtless had an economic as well as an emotional impact, especially on emancipated women with children. Women comprised about two- thirds of the adult field laborers Washington owned. Some of them were unmarried or married to dower slaves. Presumably, their work experiences did not change significantly, despite their free status. The circumstances in which they found themselves and the realities of a rural economy dictated that they continue to labor in the fields as they had while in bondage. Hence, emancipated mothers who chose to test their newly acquired freedom faced the challenge of providing for their children alone with only their skills as field laborers to sustain them.[18] Their free status likely afforded them little more economically than their kin in bondage.

Some of those manumitted chose to maintain close ties with Mount Vernon for many years, since Washington's will provided for the establishment of "a regular and permanent fund" for the support of those enslaved people "who from old age or bodily infirmities" lacked the ability to care for themselves.[19] The will entitled as many as 26 former slaves to support, but it is unclear how many of them availed themselves of this opportunity.[20] Extant records suggest that some of them resided on one or more of the outlying farms, where they received food, clothing, lodging, firewood, and medical care. Others received support while housed on a neighboring estate, or as in the case of Old Judy, in town. The last of these pensioners — Suckey, Myrtilla, Molly and Gabriel — continued to receive support as late as the 1830s. The total expense of caring for these freed people amounted to just over $10,000, paid over the years until 1833, when the last pensioner died.[21]

Among those who maintained a long-term connection to Mount Vernon was William Lee, Washington's former valet, who had received special mention in the will. Lee had been purchased in the 1760s while in his teens. He accompanied Washington to war when the Revolution commenced, and remained his body servant until a crippling injury made it difficult for him to perform such duties and necessitated his transition to cobbling shoes at the Mansion House. Washington stipulated in his will that Lee would be granted "immediate freedom" and be given the choice of leaving the plantation or remaining. In any case, he was granted "an annuity of thirty dollars during his natural life, which shall be independent of the victuals and cloaths he has been accustomed to receive, if he chuses the last alternative; but in full, with his freedom, if he prefers the first . . . ."[22] Whether guided by some sense of loyalty or simply convinced that his crippling condition would render him unable to provide for himself, Lee chose to remain at Mount Vernon until his death in the late 1820s.

Some non-pensioners maintained a degree of association with Mount Vernon as well. As late as 1835, a reporter for the *Alexandria Gazette* witnessed a group of free people of color, who identified themselves as Washington's former slaves, tending his gravesite. The 11 men and one woman included the brothers Dick and Morris Jasper, the sons of Dick and Charity, who had been laborers on the Dogue Run Farm. Dick the younger had acquired his freedom in 1800 along with his parents and his sister Tomison Gray; Morris's birth followed his parents' manumission. Levi and Joe Richardson, likely brothers as well (both had mothers named Sall or Sally who had been enslaved at the estate), were too young to have been enslaved at Mount Vernon. So was George Lear. His connection to the plantation was through his mother Rose, who doubtless was the same woman who received her emancipation along with her four children. Lear was born after she acquired her freedom. Berkley Clark (or <u>Barkley</u> Clark as listed in the Fairfax Register), had been emancipated by the provisions of Washington's will along with his mother Linney (or Ginny), and his sister Matilda. Both Joseph Smith and Nancy Quander (spelled Squander by the reporter) were former Mount Vernon slaves as well. Smith likely was the same Joe who had worked as a laborer on the Union Farm in 1799 (although there is a difference in age by a few years). Sambo Anderson, who appeared alongside his son William, had been a carpenter at the Mansion House, and had been married to the dower slave Agnes. It is unclear what ties William Hayes had to Mount Vernon; but it is possible that he was Nancy Quander's grandson, since her daughter Elizabeth was a Hayes.[23]

For those wishing to sever their ties to a servile past, residence at

Mount Vernon senior interpreter Dale Guy conducts a special guided tour on slave life at Mount Vernon.

or near Mount Vernon would have held little appeal. An urban setting like Alexandria or the new federal city would have been more to their liking. By 1820, Letty and her two (perhaps three) children manumitted with her from the Muddy Hole farm in 1801 called Alexandria home. It is unclear how early Sarah Jones had arrived in the city from Mount Vernon. At the age of 66 in 1847, when she registered in Alexandria, Sarah was probably the young woman of the same name who had labored on the Dogue Run farm in 1799. Gracey Quander, the daughter of freed woman Nancy (presumably the Nancy Quander encountered by the reporter in 1835) and Levi Jones, the son of Mount Vernon carpenter Davey and his laborer wife Evy (or Edy), both sought to make lives for themselves beyond the place that had held their parents enslaved. These free people likely settled in one of three Alexandria neighborhoods where African Americans concentrated before the Civil War: "the Bottoms," "Hay-ti," and "the Berg." Established in the aftermath of the Haitian Revolution, legend has it that the community known as Hayti took its name from that slave uprising. The Berg, located near the river, initially was called Fishtown and was the center of labor and lodging for those free people of color engaged in water-related industries.[24]

Peter Hanes, who participated at the special ceremony honoring George Washington's slaves held on January 1, 2001, is a descendant of Suckey Bay.

After the Civil War, other communities such as "the Hill," "Cross Canal," and "the Hump" attracted African Americans in search of independence and economic opportunity.[25]

Free men of color sought and acquired jobs in a number of skilled and semi-skilled capacities, including blacksmithing, carpentry, boating, teamstering, huckstering, barbering, and domestic service in the restaurants, hotels, and boarding houses. The 22 men who had labored as artisans at Mount Vernon possessed those skills that made them readily marketable in Alexandria. Others, less skilled, may have found seasonal work, especially in the water-related industries. The mermaid tattoo that decorated the arm of Letty's 23 year-old son Billy, for instance, suggests that he pursued a seafaring occupation.[26] Both black men and women in Alexandria engaged in fishing and in preparing the catch for shipment.[27] Although economic opportunity was restricted everywhere, the nature of the urban environment made it possible for the emancipated to acquire and maintain a subsistence for themselves and their families.

Towns like Alexandria also fulfilled the social needs of free people of color. Although they established mutual aid societies early on, the most significant and enduring of black social institutions was the church. Black Alexandrians founded two of them in the early 19th century: Alfred Street Baptist (which evolved from the Colored Baptist Society) and Roberts Chapel (initially named Davis Chapel and an outgrowth of Trinity Methodist).[28] Roberts Chapel became the spiritual home of the Rev. Robert Henry Robinson, the grandson of Caroline Branham, one of the dower slaves and the wife of Peter Hardman (possibly a free man). Born in 1825 in Alexandria, Robinson virtually taught himself to read and write. He engaged in various civic activities, including the opening of a night school and organizing a debating club, and he pastored several local churches in Washington, D.C., and Baltimore, in addition to Alexandria.[29]

The churches provided much more than spiritual guidance. They became centers for social events, promoted education, permitted free blacks to hone their leadership skills, and provided an avenue through which the neediest might seek assistance.[30] The repressive restrictions enforced after 1846, when Alexandria was retroceded to Virginia, frustrated the efforts of free people of color to establish much-needed social outlets, but their religious institutions permitted them to develop and maintain a strong sense of community.

Whether they made their homes in rural Fairfax County or the town settings of Alexandria and the District of Columbia, Washington's former slaves and their descendants faced the same legal, social, and political restrictions imposed on all free people of color throughout Virginia during the antebellum period. Law and custom required that they maintain a position of subordination to their white neighbors and to any other whites with whom they came into either daily or infrequent contact. The law required them to carry certificates of freedom and forced them to obtain special licenses to reside within the borders of certain towns. Free people of color could not conduct meetings or assemble, except for religious worship, and even then a white minister maintained control over the congregation. Fearing slave and free black uprisings, whites tried to deny literacy to both groups. Free blacks could not testify against whites, nor vote, nor hold public office, nor serve on juries. Their status as quasi-free people made them subject to arrest at the slightest provocation.[31]

The degree to which laws and custom circumscribed free black life depended primarily on the times. For that period when Alexandria was a part of the District of Columbia (1801-1846), whites failed to enforce the laws with any consistency. Even in Fairfax County, free people of color could and did find ways to circumvent measures designed to keep them subjugated. Despite the seeming laxity of the laws, however, blacks were forever cognizant of their tenuous status and recognized that, without warning, the goodwill of their neighbors, employers, and benefactors could give way to oppression. After Nat Turner's abortive rebellion in Southhampton County, Virginia, both enslaved and free people suffered the imposition of increasingly restrictive measures.[32]

Yet, even a few of those disadvantaged by racial prejudice managed to distinguish themselves in terms of the degree of prosperity they attained and the leadership roles they held in their respective communities. George Lewis Seaton, the eldest son of the manumitted dower slave Lucinda and her husband George Seaton, Sr., held membership in this class of elites. The elder Seatons, who reared 10 children, owned extensive real estate holdings in Alexandria. When George, Sr. died in 1845, he bequeathed that property to his wife and children.[33] The younger George's right to inclusion among the elite originated in this bequest from his father. His prosperity grew as well as a result of his skills as a master carpenter. By the age of 34 (on the eve of the Civil War), he owned real estate valued at $4,000.[34] After the war ended, Seaton continued to expand his business interests by establishing a successful grocery store and by purchasing lots and houses in Alexandria. By 1870, his real estate holdings were valued at $15,000; and at the time of his death in 1889, he was considerably wealthier with holdings purportedly valued at nearly $100,000.[35]

It was during the immediate postwar years that Seaton took his place among the black leadership of the newly developing community of free born and freed people. He assisted in the establishment of a building association in Alexandria in the 1860s, helped to found the Colored YMCA and was elected its president in 1873. In the meantime, he became a member of the Alfred Street Baptist Church and served as trustee of the Colored Odd Fellows Association. Considering his prominence in the African-American community, it seems inevitable that Seaton would become involved in Reconstruction politics. He actively participated in the various Republican Clubs then forming in Alexandria, and served as a delegate to the Republican Convention held in Richmond in 1867. In 1869, Alexandrians elected him to represent them in the House of Delegates at the first session of the General Assembly which had been convened after Virginia's readmission to the Union. After one term, he returned home where he served on the city council.[36]

Apparently George was not the only descendant of Lucinda to attain success. There is some indication that William Calvin Chase, the founder and publisher of the *Washington Bee*, descended from the former Mount Vernon slave as well. We know little about Chase's mother, Lucinda Seaton, except that she had a brother named John A. A Chase biographer deduced that George L. Seaton must have been Lucinda's uncle or father. More probably, he was her brother, since Lucinda and George Seaton, Sr., had a son named John Andrew and a daughter named Lucinda.[37]

Sometime in the early 1850s Lucinda Seaton (the younger) married William H. Chase, a blacksmith and wheelwright in the District of Columbia. For the next decade the couple lived comfortably with their six children and became members of the Fifteenth Street Presbyterian Church. After her husband's death in 1863 from an assailant's bullet, Lucinda reared her children with income she earned as a dressmaker. She maintained her prominence in the community by becoming politically active and, along with her daughters, joined the National Suffrage Association. Some of the most prominent black civic leaders of the last quarter of the 19th century gathered in her home, including Henry Highland Garnet, the militant former abolitionist and fiery advocate of equality for the freed people; Blanche K. Bruce, Reconstruction senator from Mississippi; John Mercer Langston, sole black member of the House of Representatives from Virginia during the 19th century; and Ida B. Wells-Barnett, crusader for federal anti-lynching legislation. In 1882,

Lucinda's son, William, founded the *Bee*, whose slogan was "Honey for friends, stings for enemies." Just before the turn of the century, he received admission to the judicial bar after having graduated from the Howard University Law School. At least three of his five sisters became teachers.[38]

Although less conspicuously successful than the Seatons, the Jones family traced its roots at Mount Vernon to two of Washington's former slaves. Davy and Evy (sometimes spelled Eby) acquired their freedom in 1801, along with their two daughters — six-year-old Sarah and one-year-old Nancy. The family eventually grew to include three sons — David, Joseph, and Levi. When the children registered with Fairfax County in 1831, they referenced Davy and Evy in their individual claims to free status.[39]

Apparently dissatisfied with the opportunities (or lack thereof) in rural Fairfax, Levi Jones migrated to Alexandria by the early 1840s. Soon thereafter, he became a property owner, acquiring 14 acres of land in 1844 with a down payment of $200 and an additional $235 to be paid over a period of five years. By the time the Civil War commenced, Jones's farm consisted of 17 acres, 12 of which had been cleared for cultivation.[40] Jones's property eventually became the southern extension of the Nauck community, a settlement which grew out of the post-Civil War sale of parcels of land to groups of freed people who had initially settled at Freedman's Village, where were housed some of the thousands of fugitives who escaped to the Union lines during the war. In the early stages of the community's development, Jones's home served as school, church, and meeting house. When he died in 1886, his property remained in the family, under the control of his wife Sarah and their five children.[41]

The Quanders claimed one of the eight Nancys who lived and labored contemporaneously at Mount Vernon before Washington's death. In 1831, 20-year-old Gracey Quander registered with Fairfax County and established her freedom by virtue of the emancipation of her mother Nancy by Washington's will. Her sister, Elizabeth, five years her junior, registered in 1836. Nancy, herself, failed to register in either Fairfax or Alexandria County. Apparently, she still lived in the area in 1831, since the *Gazette* reporter found her among those tending the grave of Washington just four years later.[42]

Little else is known of Nancy, including whether she acquired the name Quander through marriage or by birth. It is unclear at present how she relates to other people of color of the same surname who resided in Maryland and Virginia in the 18th and 19th centuries. The descendants of those two groups excelled as independent farmers, and later, as educators.[43]

As with the Quanders, the Holland family claims descent from a resident among the enslaved population at Mount Vernon; but proof of a connection has been elusive. Oral tradition has allowed the family to trace their ancestry at least to William Holland who they believed was born in 1822. Unfortunately, when Holland registered with the Fairfax County court in 1847 and again in 1852, he provided no information regarding parentage, citing only an affidavit that confirmed his free status through birth. Moreover, none of the many Hollands listed in the Fairfax register or in Alexandria indicate the process by which they acquired their freedom.[44]

Despite their inability to provide concrete proof of a connection to Washington's laborers, certain circumstantial evidence makes the Holland claim credible. By the late 19th century, the family was firmly established in the Gum Springs community (a settlement occupied primarily by post-Civil War freed people), after having been settled for many years at nearby Woodlawn (home of Custis heir Eleanor Parke Custis Lewis).[45] As early as 1856 William Holland had purchased 28 acres of land in the Woodlawn area from the Quaker, Chalkley Gillingham, and his wife Kezaiel, for $450.[46] Gillingham, his brother Lucas, and Jacob and Paul Hillman Troth — all partners in a lumber business — had purchased Woodlawn in the late 1840s, with the intention of cutting the timber on the 2,000-acre estate and selling it to shipbuilders. A second motive — the establishment of farms cultivated with the use of free labor — reflected an attempt on the part of the Quakers to convince Virginians of the advantage and feasibility of freeing their slaves and employing them as wage laborers.[47] Holland's land purchase fit well with their plans.

In 1877, the rather prosperous Holland gave testimony before the Southern Claims Commission, an agency established in the years following the Civil War to handle claims resulting from the Union army's appropriation of private property during the war. William Holland filed claim for reimbursement for goods that had been seized when Union soldiers crossed over his land in February 1862. Asserting that he remained loyal to the Union throughout the war, Holland testified that he "never had no taste for the Confederate side" and had joined the Union Home Guard raised at Accotink, Virginia. As the law required, he produced witnesses who attested to his loyalty and to his ownership of the appropriated property. One of those witnesses, P. Hillman Troth (Gillingham's partner in the lumber business) testified that Holland was "a smart intelligent, black man; his mother belonged to Gen Washington."[48] Unfortunately, neither Troth nor any of the other witnesses testifying for Holland provided the mother's name.

In any case, the Hollands also established a long-term association with Mount Vernon through employment. Family members such as William Warren Holland worked at the estate well into the twentieth century. William Warren's labor there began in 1903, and continued for the next 60 years or more. In 1936, he received promotion to a post some considered a position of honor during that time: "keeper of the tomb" or tomb guard.[49] Legend has it that the post was reserved for the descendants of the Mount Vernon slaves.

An equally intriguing (if less convincing) example of claim of a connection to emancipated laborers at Mount Vernon is the case of Richard Stanhope (or Stanup) of Urbana, Ohio. The oral tradition in Stanhope's family suggests that he was "chief of the slaves" and had served as Washington's valet during the Revolutionary War. When Washington died, Stanhope allegedly was freed and received a 400-acre land grant in Champaign County, Ohio, as a token of appreciation for faithful service. In 1958, the Urbana Chapter of the Daughters of the American Revolution erected a marker on his grave which read "Valet during the American Revolution and faithful chief of servants for General George Washington at Mount Vernon."[50]

Extant records provide no clues to Richard Stanhope's identity. No one of his description appears on the 1799 inventory. Nor is there any indication that Washington had any body servant other than William Lee until after the latter was incapacitated in the 1790s. Lee's position fell eventually to a young Mount Vernon slave named Christopher.[51]

One of the most documented and best known enslaved residents at Mount Vernon came to the estate after the death of George Washington. West Ford, the son of enslaved woman Venus, attracted the attention of Hannah Bushrod Washington, the widow of the former president's brother John Augustine. In an unusual move, Hannah Washington made provisions for the child's inoculation against smallpox and stipulated that he be "bound to a good tradesman until the age of 21 years after which he is to be free the rest of his life."[52] Ford eventually labored for Hannah's son Bushrod, who served as executor of Washington's estate. When Bushrod died in 1829, he willed 160 acres of land to the former slave. Through ingenuity and business acumen, Ford purchased 211 acres with the money earned from sale of the bequest. These holdings made him the first black owner of the land that eventually became Gum Springs. His care in securing this land for his heirs by subdividing it before his death ensured that other African Americans — both free born and newly emancipated — would enter the ranks of the land owning.[53]

For now, we know too little about the experiences of the former slaves who resided at Mount Vernon to offer any substantive conclusions about the group as a whole. The emerging picture of the emancipated and their children thus far, however — notwithstanding Custis's indictment of their performance in freedom — is that some of them enjoyed success far greater than one would have expected, given their humble beginnings and the realities of living as free people of color in a slave society. Despite proscriptions imposed on them, some succeeded in rearing children who, in the post-Civil War years, commanded the respect of whites as well as fellow African Americans and ascended to the highest levels of leadership in their communities. If the majority of the emancipated remain virtually anonymous today, perhaps it is so because they intended it. If they had wanted notoriety, they could have adopted the Washington appellation as their own. It is perhaps no coincidence that none of those who registered as free people in Fairfax and Alexandria in the decades before the Civil War chose to embrace the most famous name in the area.

Notes

The author wishes to thank the following persons for their generous sharing of documents and time: Mary Thompson, Audrey Davis, Sean Costly, Robert Holland, Guinevere Jones, Anna Lynch, Lillian Patterson, Michi Gresham, David Terry and Craig Evans. Champaign County, Ohio, Historical Society.

1. John C. Fitzpatrick, ed., *The Writings of George Washington from the Original Manuscript Sources, 1745-1799*, 39 vols. (Washington, D.C., 1944), 37:276-77.
2. George Washington Parke Custis, *Recollections and Memoirs of Washington* (Washington, D.C., 1859), 12. For discussion of the slaves at Mount Vernon see Gloria L. Smith, *Black Americana at Mount Vernon: Genealogy Techniques for Slave Group Research* (Tucson, 1984).
3. For instance, naming patterns at Mount Vernon led to the contemporaneous existence of eight different Nancys.
4. Fritz Hirschfeld, *George Washington and Slavery: A Documentary Portrayal* (Columbia, Mo., 1997), 19.
5. *Writings*, 37:256-268.
6. For discussion of the laws in effect at the time Washington drew up his will see Frank Morse, "About General Washington's Freed Negroes," unpublished essay, Mount Vernon Estate Library, 1968.
7. *Writings*, 37:276.
8. James Thomas Flexner, *Washington, the Indispensable Man* (Boston, 1974), 393. Abigail Adams indicated that Martha Washington freed her husband's slaves early because she feared that they would plot her demise.
9. Dorothy S. Provine, ed., *Alexandria County, Virginia Free Negro Registers, 1797-1861*, 3 vols. (Bowie, Maryland, 1990), 1:99.
10. *Writings*, 37:259.
11. Provine, *Alexandria County, Virginia Free Negro Registers*, 1 (Registration # 206b, May 28, 1827).
12. See Alexandria Court House Deed Book E (1803), 153.
13. The Alexandria County Register and similar volumes for Fairfax County provide valuable assistance in the effort to identify the emancipated; and they offer clues as well to where the former slaves eventually settled. Two of the three volumes of the Fairfax Counter register, discovered in 1974, were indexed and

edited three years later by Donald Sweig of the Fairfax County Office of Comprehensive Planning. The two volumes cover the years from 1822 to 1861. The three-volume set of registers for Alexandria County, abstracted and indexed by Dorothy Provine, covers the period from 1797-1861.

14. Donald Sweig, ed., *Registrations of Free Negroes Commencing September Court 1822*, Book No. 2 and *Register of Free Blacks, 1835*, Book 3" (Fairfax, Va., 1977), 96.

15. Sweig, *Registration of Free Negroes*, Book 2, 11, and Book 3, 118.

16. Elijah Blackburn, 20, and Harrison Backburn, 22, claimed freedom through Washington's will on November 20, 1837. See Sweig, *Registration of Free Negroes*, Book 2, 117.

17. *Writings*, 37:256-268.

18. *Writings*, 37:256-268. See also Eugene Prussing, *The Estate of George Washington, Deceased* (Boston, 1927); Frank Morse, "About General Washington's Freed Negroes," 3.

19. *Writings*, 37:276. Virginia law required financial support for formerly enslaved people of certain ages. *The Statutes at Large of Virginia: Being a Collection of All the Laws of Virginia from the First Session of the Legislature in the Year 1619*, ed. William Waller Hening, 13 vols. (Richmond, 1809-23), 11:39.

20. See Frank Morse, "About General Washington's Freed Negroes."

21. Eugene Prussing, *The Estate of George Washington, Deceased*. See also Frank Morse, "About General Washington's Freed Negroes," 3. Items from the Executors' Account Book (published in Prussing) indicate that some freed blacks were cared for although not entitled to benefits by the provisions of the will.

22. Fritz Hirschfeld, *George Washington and Slavery: A Documentary Portrayal*, 108.

23. Gloria Smith, *Black Americana at Mount Vernon*, 48. See also Donald Sweig, *Registrations of Free Negroes* for some of these people, as well as the 1799 inventory in *Writings*, 37.

24. Nan Netherton et al., *Fairfax County, Virginia: A History* (Fairfax, Va., 1978), 275-76. See also Elsa S. Rosenthal, "1790 Names - 1970 Faces: A Short History of Alexandria's Slave and Free Black Community," in Elizabeth Hambleton and Marian Van Landingham, ed., *Alexandria: A Composite History* (Alexandria, Va., 1975), 87.

25. Few free people of color resided in Alexandria County in 1800; the 383 who did comprised approximately six percent of the overall population, three times fewer than the percentage of slaves. By 1860, free blacks had reached 11 percent, and they were about equal to the percentage of slaves at the time. The vast majority of free blacks lived in the town of Alexandria rather than the county. Federal census returns for Virginia indicate that the population of town and county was reported separately from 1810 to 1840. See also Dorothy Provine, *Alexandria County, Virginia Free Negro Registers*, 1:x.

26. Anna Lynch, *A Compendium of Early African Americans in Alexandria, Virginia* (2 vols., Alexandria, 1995-96), 1:6. A third volume of the Lynch compendium is scheduled for publication.

27. Elsa S. Rosenthal, "1790 Names - 1970 Faces," 87; Nan Netherton, *Fairfax*

County, Virginia: A History, 276.

28. United States Department of the Interior, National Park Service, National Register of Historic Places, "Alexandria's African American Heritage," Section E, p. 14. Copy on file at the Alexandria Black History Resource Center.

29. Magnus Lewis Robinson, *Sketches of the Life of Truman Pratt, the Centenarian, Including the History of Orchard Street M.E. Church, Baltimore, Md.*, 20; and *Fiftieth Anniversary Souvenir Program for Roberts Memorial United Methodist Church*, May 12, 1990.

30. Elsa S. Rosenthal, "1790 Names - 1970 Faces, 89; Harold W. Hurst, *Alexandria on the Potomac: The Portrait of an Antebellum Community* (Lanham, Md., 1991), 39-40.

31. June Purcell Guild, *Black Laws of Virginia: A Summary of the Legislative Acts of Virginia Concerning Negroes from Earliest Times to the Present* (Richmond, 1936); *Code of Virginia, Including Legislation to the Year 1860* (Richmond, 1860; reprint Westport, Conn., 1970). See also Elsa S. Rosenthal, "1790 Names-1970 Faces," 86-87; and Harold Hurst, *Alexandria on the Potomac*, 37-38.

32. Donald Sweig, "Free and Black in Northern Virginia <u>Before</u> the Civil War," *Northern Virginia Heritage Magazine* 5, no.1 (February, 1983), 4-5; and Elsa S. Rosenthal, "1790 Names -1970 Faces," 85.

33. "Will of George Seaton," Will Book, Orphans Court, No. 4, Alexandria County, Virginia, 387-390.

34. T. Michael Miller, ed., *Alexandria, Virginia: City and County Census, 1860* (Bowie, Md., 1986), 106.

35. Harold Hurst, *Alexandria on the Potomac*, 38. See also Penny Morrill, *Who Built Alexandria?: Architects in Alexandria, 1750-1900* (Alexandria, Va., 1979), 32-33.

36. Luther Porter Jackson, *Negro Officeholders in Virginia, 1865-1895* (Norfolk, 1942), 38; see also Penny Morrill, *Who Built Alexandria?*, 32-33.

37. See Hal Scripps Chase, "Honey for Friends, Stings for Enemies: William Calvin Chase and the Washington Bee, 1822-1921" (Ph.D. diss., University of Pennsylvania, 1973). Chase concluded, incorrectly, that George L. Seaton was Lucinda Seaton Chase's father or uncle because, apparently, he had not been aware of the Alexandria Registers of Free Blacks, which in 1841 listed George L., John A., and Lucinda as members of the same family.

38. Hal Scripps Chase, "'Honey for Friends,'" 1-20.

39. Donald Sweig, *Registrations of Free Negroes*, Book 2, 66, 96 and 98.

40. Deposition of Levi Jones of Alexandria County, Virginia, before the Southern Claims Commission, Southern Claims Case Files, 1877-88, Third Auditor's Office, Virginia, Claim #12,805 (43,014), December 4, 1876, RG 217, National Archives. According to the Southern Claims Commission Records, Jones had purchased all 17 acres from "the Widow Bagot . . . ." A deed dated October 1844 indicates that Jones purchased 14 acres from Elizabeth Baggot. It is unclear how he acquired the money for the purchase.

41. Thomas O'Brien, "Historic Survey of Nauck Neighborhood, Arlington County, Va.," December, 1987, unpublished essay in the Nauck File, Arlington County

Library; Interview with Sean Costley of Alexandria (descendent of Levi Jones), September, 1994.

42. Donald Sweig, *Registrations of Free Negroes*, Book 2, 63; Book 3, 113.

43. The Quanders United Incorporated, *The Quanders United Tricentennial Celebration: 1684-1984* (Washington, D.C., 1984).

44. Donald Sweig, *Registrations of Free Negroes...*, Book 3, pp. 158 and 204.

45. The bulk of Gum Springs residents were newly emancipated blacks who settled there in the post-Civil War years.

46. William Holland from Kezaiel and Chalkley Gillingham, 6 December, 1856, Fairfax County Deed Book, 1856, H-8-225.

47. Nan Netherton et al., *Fairfax County, Virginia: A History*, 258.

48. Deposition of P. Hillman Troth for William Holland of Fairfax County, Virginia, April 5, 1877, Southern Claims Case Files, #17091.

49. Elswyth Thane, *Mount Vernon – The Legacy: The Story of Its Preservation and Care Since 1885* (Philadelphia, 1967), 49.

50. For a discussion of Stanhope's claims see, "Urbana Man's Great-Grandfather was Washington's Personal Valet," *News-Sun*, (Springfield, Oh.), 1987.

51. Fritz Hirschfeld, *George Washington and Slavery: A Documentary Portrayal*, 107.

52. Judith Saunders-Burton, "A History of Gum Springs, Virginia: A Report of a Case Study of Leadership in a Black Enclave" (D. Ed. diss., Vanderbilt University, 1986). See also Donald Sweig, "Free and Black in Northern Virginia," 6.

53. Judith Saunders-Burton, "A History of Gum Springs, Virginia."

This monument to the Mount Vernon slaves was erected by the Mount Vernon Ladies' Association in 1929 near the burial site of approximately 50 slaves and free blacks. At the time, it was thought to be the first memorial of its kind in the United States.

Looking Back, Moving Forward: The Changing Interpretation of Slave Life on the Mount Vernon Estate

James C. Rees

"Tear those buildings down."

These four words of advice marked the first of many controversial decisions related to the issue of slavery that would be faced by the Mount Vernon Ladies' Association.

In the years after the Association assumed ownership of the Mansion and 200 acres in 1858, several trusted advisors to Ann Pamela Cunningham, the Association's founder and first Regent, recommended that the plantation's outbuildings be destroyed. Because most of these structures were where slaves both worked and lived, they served as a constant reminder of slavery, which was the cause of the wrenchingly painful Civil War. Throughout the 1860s and 1870s, as a nation divided tried to heal old wounds, the argument persisted — these buildings recalled far too much misery and suffering, not only by the slaves themselves, but by Civil War soldiers from both North and South.

Miss Cunningham never explained in detail the reasons why she ignored this advice, but the outbuildings remained intact. In her farewell address to fellow board members, she wrote that the "mansion, and the grounds around it, should be religiously guarded from changes — should be kept as Washington left them."[1]

In all likelihood, Miss Cunningham's decision reflected her unshakable belief in protecting history, pure and simple. Clearly, she was ahead of her time. It would be decades before a national preservation movement would take the country by storm, and more than 90 years until this movement would be consolidated with the formation of the National Trust for Historic Preservation.

As a southerner who witnessed the effects of the Civil War on her own plantation in South Carolina, it is unlikely that she envisioned slavery as a topic destined to be interpreted at

159

Washington's estate. Association records reveal that the original Regent and Vice Regents focused the lion's share of their attention on restoring and refurbishing the Mansion. The messages delivered to visitors seldom strayed from George Washington. Mount Vernon was referred to again and again as a national shrine, and Washington's role as a slave owner was one that was at best ignored, and at times defended.

Yet visitors to Mount Vernon, if not confronted with the controversy surrounding slavery, were constantly reminded that Washington's plantation was home to both whites and blacks. A number of descendants of the African Americans who worked for Washington at Mount Vernon were enlisted as gardeners, spinners, weavers and guards, according to Harrison Howell Dodge, who served as Resident Director of Mount Vernon from 1885 until 1937.[2]

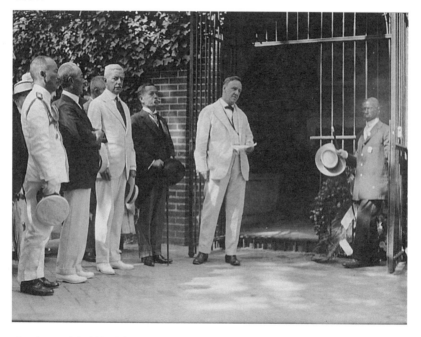

On August 26, 1917, Mount Vernon welcomed a host of dignitaries from Japan, as well as Roland S. Morris, the U.S. Ambassador to Japan. At the wreathlaying ceremony at George Washington's Tomb, Charles F. Simms, the long-time guard at the tomb, made sure that all participants removed their hats before the ceremony began.

When the memoirs of Colonel Dodge were published in 1932, the bicentennial of Washington's birth, a chapter was devoted to "The Old Negroes" who worked on the estate.[3] Dodge makes several references to Charles F. Simms, who traveled to Mount Vernon from Leesburg, Virginia, in 1913, to assume the post of guard at George Washington's tomb. Dodge noted that Simms "upheld a sort of tradition of behavior and attitude that has been passed on from generation to generation among the colored men and women at Mount Vernon, inherited by the older ones, absorbed by the newer, so that it indeed appears to be true that they are the living links between the fevered present and the storied past."[4]

Dodge credits "the good memories of many of the old Negroes for information concerning the former location and condition of various structures and growing things on the estate."[5] In a time when the standards of preservation and restoration were far less stringent, these memories often took the place of in-depth research and extensive archaeological investigations.

Simms took his job quite seriously, and his reverence for George Washington seems to have been deeply felt. Dodge reports that Simms was called upon to maintain a sense of decorum at Washington's burial site. With some frequency, Simms asked visitors to stop smoking and to maintain a church-like sense of tranquility. Gentlemen were asked to "kindly remove" their hats.[6]

Although most of Dodge's recollections are warm and complimentary, at least by 1930s standards, there are a few references that reflect the underlying racism and tension that existed, even in the non-threatening environment of the Mount Vernon estate. A confrontation occurred when a man asked by Simms to remove his hat "passionately resented the interference with his personal liberty and hotly declared he was a Virginian and 'didn't allow a nigger to attempt to teach him good manners.'"[7] Dodge goes on to tell of a second incident, when King Albert of Belgium visited the tomb in 1918, attired in full military regalia, including an impressive hat. When Simms "whispered tastefully" to the King, "Your cap, Sir," the royal visitor complied without protest.[8]

Dodge describes another African American who served in the

tomb position, Edon Hammond, as a "sensitive" man with a "strong voice and grandiloquent style." He delivered colorful welcomes at the tomb and "enthralled his attentive audience."[9] Encouraged by grateful visitors, Hammond created a text of his presentation and printed a pamphlet for circulation on the estate, without the official sanction of Dodge or the Mount Vernon board. When he was told the pamphlet could not be distributed, Hammond quit in protest.

In Dodge's book, he includes what appears to be a portion of Hammond's lecture, which he notes "went somewhat as follows:"

> For while the Capitol stands only on one corner of the victory gained by General Washington, he stands the center of veneration in each State. He who stood on the field of battle for eight consecutive years, a well-tried target, and from whose coat five buttons were shot, without a wound penetrating his body. That he might bring home an incalculable amount of freedom, together with an unmeasurable boundary of union, to be distributed among the sons and daughters of the United States of America, and not to them only, but to as many as thought proper to come from distant lands and beyond the seas. All of whom were made welcome participants, without discrimination or preventation. Therefore this spot is the center of attraction in the realm of veneration, to all true patriotic historians, who love freedom and venerate union.[10]

Since Hammond's own version of his lecture does not survive, it is difficult to know whether this excerpt is a fair representation of his remarks, or whether Dodge is blending the sentiments of Hammond with those of his own.

After reading Dodge's memoirs, with their consistently condescending tone, it would appear that the buildings at Mount Vernon were not the only aspects of 18th-century life that were being preserved. The African Americans who worked at Mount Vernon, though appreciated for their memories of yesteryear and their diligence on the job, were still employed in the most subservient positions on the estate. In many ways, the atmosphere at Mount Vernon was a microcosm of the nation in general, particularly in the South. More than a century after Washington died and his slaves were set free, equality between the races still had a long way to go.

There were times, however, when the Association continued to break new ground. True to Ann Pamela Cunningham's original refusal to sweep slavery under the carpet, the Mount Vernon board made a forward-thinking decision in 1928 to recognize and commemorate the slave burial ground.[11] Located just 50 yards from the Washington Family Tomb, this shaded area above the Potomac River was where some 50 African Americans, both free and enslaved, were placed at rest.[12]

In the official minutes of the 1928 annual meeting of the Association, the chairman of the Tomb Committee, Frances C. Maxey from Texas, reported to the board: "The graveyard which was used by General Washington for his slaves is unmarked. In the course of time, it is possible that all traces of the graves will disappear. It is recommended that a simple marker, suitably inscribed, be placed on this consecrated ground."[13]

At the same meeting, Annie B. Jennings, the Vice Regent for Connecticut, offered to contribute funds to support the purchase of the memorial stone.[14] A year later, a single piece of Georgian marble was placed at the edge of the burial ground, with the following inscription: "In memory of the many faithful colored servants of the Washington family buried at Mount Vernon from 1760 to 1800. Their unidentified graves surround this spot."[15] As simple as this tribute may be, the action was unprecedented. For the next 50 years, this marker would remain the only official memorial to 18th-century slaves at an American historic site.

This is not to say that the slave burial ground became a popular part of a visit to the Mount Vernon estate. There are very few references to the memorial or burial ground in the minutes of the Association, and the official handbook to the estate, sold to tens of thousands of visitors, ignored the site for some five decades to follow.

In the late 30s, 40s and 50s, the issue of slavery again rose to the forefront as the Association made plans to restore Washington's greenhouse structure, which also provided quarters to a number of slaves. Washington constructed the greenhouse in the late 1780s. The slave quarters, which were added in 1792, housed approximately 60 slaves, including men, women and children.

Washington's greenhouse and slave quarters structure was destroyed by fire on a bitter winter night in 1835. When the Association purchased the estate 23 years later, little evidence remained of the original structure.[16] Only after some old insurance records were uncovered, and a careful analysis was conducted of the many references Washington made to slavery in his writings, did the Association feel it could rebuild the structure with any degree of authenticity. The reconstruction took place over a period of years, and coincided with a major renovation at The White House during the Truman presidency. In fact, when a number of original White House bricks were deemed surplus during the renovation process, they were shipped to Mount Vernon for use in the greenhouse reconstruction — a gift from one presidential home to another.

An interesting contradiction arose when Mount Vernon's researchers studied existing records to determine the interior configuration of the slave quarters. In April 1792, the weekly work reports of Washington's manager referred to carpenters and bricklayers working on the construction of berths.[17] Apparently, these were simple planks on brick foundations, one bunk placed above the other. Research at other period plantations has uncovered few references to barracks-style quarters in the late 18th century, although the practice was far more common on large plantations earlier in the century.

Because a large number of occupants shared such a modest space, the staff of the Association made the judgment that "bunks would have been a practical solution to the problem of accommodating this number of people."[18] Washington often expressed a certain level of frustration in his efforts to manage the slaves at the Mansion House Farm, and perhaps the barracks were an attempt to encourage a sense of order. It may also be true that Washington may have become an advocate of barracks-style living during his tenure as commander in chief in the Revolutionary War. After almost a decade of research and discussion, the west quarter was furnished to reflect this configuration and has remained in a similar format for the past 40 years.

When the finished slave quarter was finally opened to the public

Howard University Dean Harry Robinson and three members of the winning team of student architects of the Mount Vernon Slave Memorial.

on George Washington's 230th birthday, February 22, 1962, it was one of the first and most important depictions of slave life ever completed.[19] In hindsight, however, its authenticity remains in doubt. With one adult per berth, the existing layout would accommodate only ten people. But if Washington did indeed house as many as 60 slaves in this building, and this room represents almost a quarter of the living space, it would seem that each room would need to serve as a sleeping area for many more people. It is also questionable whether Washington would have allowed his carpenters to spend their time fashioning shaped headboards and finials to adorn furniture used by slaves.

It is disappointing that the three other rooms used by Washington as residential spaces for slaves were not restored, but rather converted to modern usages. Today, a retail shop, a restroom for handicapped visitors, a small museum focusing on archaeology and restoration, and assorted storage spaces are located where dozens of slaves lived in the 18th century.

For the next two decades, little else was done to focus attention on the life of slaves on the Mount Vernon estate, despite the fact that the civil rights movement was in full swing. Scholarship on slavery had begun to blossom in both Europe and America, but historic sites in general, including Mount Vernon, were not rushing to change their perspectives.

Meanwhile, the path to the 1929 slave marker had become so overgrown that visitors were unaware it even existed. Many staff members considered the marker a stop on a "behind-the-scenes tour" of Mount Vernon.[20] A turning point occurred in 1982 and 1983 when Dorothy Gilliam, a regular columnist with the *Washington Post*, penned a series of articles criticizing the Association for its lack of care and concern for the slave marker, as well as its failure "to note black contributions to Mount Vernon."[21]

Reactions to Gilliam's words were strong and swift. James Scott, a member of the Fairfax County Board of Supervisors, discussed the issue with Frank Matthews, a professor at George Mason University and legal counsel to the Fairfax County NAACP. At a meeting of the full Board of Supervisors, Matthews argued against the Association's request for an extension of its tax-exempt status. As Gilliam reported in a column in February 1983: "The Board of Supervisors agreed, and decided to withhold tax-exempt status until a pledge was made to work with the NAACP and come up with an appropriate memorialization."[22]

Even before the pressure was applied by county officials, the Association recreated a gravel path to the slave burial ground and installed benches to encourage visitors to pause and reflect. In subsequent meetings with African-American community leaders, it was decided to move forward on a much larger project — the creation of a contemporary memorial to the enslaved residents of the Mount Vernon estate.

Judith Sanders Burton, a descendant of West Ford, a slave who moved to Mount Vernon after Washington's death, rallied the local community of Gum Springs, an area where a number of

George Washington's attractive greenhouse was also a slave quarters. The structure burned down on a bitterly cold night in 1835 and was not reconstructed until the presidency of Harry Truman.

Washington's slaves established homes after they were granted their freedom. She was joined by Dr. William Carr, a respected psychology professor.

In a series of meetings with Mount Vernon board members and staff, a plan was developed to design and construct an appropriate memorial. A competition was mounted at the Howard University School of Architecture and Planning under the supervision of Dean Harry G. Robinson. Several teams of students competed against each other, and a committee of five — Matthews, Carr, Burton, the Regent (Frances C. Guy) and the Regent-Elect (Helen S. Anderson) of the Association — were selected to serve as the competition jury.

The winning design, created by a team of ten headed by David Edge, features a brick archway and tree-lined path leading to a set of three circles, one inside another, featuring the words "faith, hope, and love." In the center is a granite column cut at an angle, inscribed with the words, "In memory of the Afro-Americans who served as slaves at Mount Vernon." After some strained discussions, the committee agreed to leave the original slave marker *in situ*, but to add the date of its placement, 1929.[23]

The official dedication of the new memorial took place on September 21, 1983. The program at the new slave memorial featured remarks by Virginia Governor Charles S. Robb and Dr. James Turner, a professor at Cornell University, among many others. The Howard University Choir provided music for the occasion, which was followed by a luncheon on the east lawn.[24]

At the same time, the Association published a brochure on the African-American slaves at Mount Vernon. Interpretive signs used at several outbuildings near the Mansion were redrafted to reflect the role of slaves in everyday plantation life. Two years later, a new draft

The restoration of the interior of the slave quarters was a long and tedious effort, but once completed, it became one of the most important slave-related projects in the nation.

of the official Mount Vernon Handbook would include material on slaves and their contributions to Washington's estate.

Many of those who banded together in the local community to fight for the creation of the Slave Memorial decided to form a new group, the Gum Springs Historical Society. Chartered in 1985, the Society seeks to preserve the heritage, culture, artifacts and traditions of the Gum Springs community. Under the leadership of Ronald L. Chase, longtime president, the Society has organized oral history workshops, genealogical seminars, and special exhibitions, which effectively communicate the important roles of African Americans in the development of Fairfax County.[25]

In 1987, the Association's search for clues about slave life at Mount Vernon would receive its most important boost to date, with the formation of a full-fledged Department of Archaeology. One of the earliest and most productive excavations was the site of the house for slave families, which Washington ultimately removed from the north lane of the estate in 1792. Excavators uncovered a trash-filled cellar that spanned some six feet and extended five feet below the earth's surface, and that contained thousands of period objects associated with the everyday lives of slaves. As other related digs were completed, it became clear that Mount Vernon possessed tens of thousands of bits and pieces that together make up the complex puzzle of 18th-century slave life on a Virginia plantation.

Research into the lives of slaves was further enhanced in 1991 when the W. K. Kellogg Foundation agreed to support the creation of a new living-history site based on Washington's leadership in the field of agriculture. Student interns were enlisted from the most important university agricultural programs in the nation. Using detailed research materials developed by Mary Thompson and other members of the Mount Vernon collections staff, the interns stepped into the shoes of 18th-century farm workers, the vast majority of whom were slaves. Visitors to the Pioneer Farm site are invited to participate in the tasks slaves were expected to accomplish from sun-up to sun-down, including the treading of wheat and the plowing of fields. They taste some of the incredibly simple — and generally unappetizing — foods that were staples for slaves. Today, most visitors to Mount Vernon are invited to taste a freshly-made hoe cake, cooked over an open fire.

Simultaneously, the interpretive staff at Mount Vernon developed a special training program to support the creation of daily slave life tours. Because these guided tours are generally small and intensive, they offer a special opportunity to delve far deeper into life at Mount Vernon. Specific slaves, such as Hercules the cook, Davy the overseer, and Caroline, Mrs. Washington's personal servant, became important representatives of a population which was far more diverse than the average visitor expects. Visitors have commented that their most memorable experience at Mount Vernon was a slave life tour conducted by Gladys Tancil, a descendant of Nancy Quander, who was the daughter of Suckey Bay, a slave who lived on River Farm. Mrs. Tancil has worked at Mount Vernon for 26 years, and her personal insights are both enlightening and moving.

In the fall of 1994, the Association sponsored a two-day conference entitled "Slavery in the Age of Washington," which included a series of formal presentations and panel discussions. A room full of historians and educators previewed the slave life tour and offered a long list of constructive criticisms.

Slavery also became a focus of the activities offered to children (and parents) in the popular Hands-On History Tent, where children learn about tools of the period, try their hands at everyday farm chores like harnessing a mule, and dress in reproduction clothing.

In 1995, Mount Vernon introduced its first audio program to the general public, featuring a personal tour of the outbuildings conducted by an enslaved bricklayer named Tom Davis. The tape describes not only the activities that took place in the busy community surrounding the Mansion, but how the residents of this community interacted with each other and with members of the Washington family.

As the century came to a close, Mount Vernon expanded its interpretive program to include a variety of first person characters who interact with visitors as they tour the estate. Dale Guy, a retired Air Force officer who joined Mount Vernon's staff in 1996, has portrayed both Hercules, Washington's sometimes temperamental

Award-winning actress Cicely Tyson is among the special wreathlayers who have participated in the annual program honoring the slaves who lived and worked at Mount Vernon. Also pictured are Sheila Coates, Founder and President of Black Women United for Action, and Lisa Moore, Vice Regent for Virginia of the Mount Vernon Ladies' Association.

cook, and Christopher Sheels, Washington's personal valet. Again, the most important aspect of this program is its focus on an individual who, like Washington himself, called Mount Vernon home.

In 1999, Mount Vernon partnered with Jackdaw Publications in Anawalk, New York, to distribute a hands-on classroom exercise entitled *Archaeology and Slave Life at Mount Vernon*. Using a variety of artifacts discovered by Mount Vernon archaeologists, high school students are challenged to compare and contrast the lifestyles of Washington family members, a hired white servant, a slave who worked in the relatively privileged environment of the Mansion House Farm, and a slave who worked in the fields of an outlying farm.

These educational initiatives, both within Mount Vernon's gates and in classrooms across the nation, have been praised by both the general public and the academic community. This is not to imply that the last decade has passed without controversy. In 1999, following on the heels of the heated debate over Thomas Jefferson's relationship with Sally Hemings, several descendants of West Ford announced that their family's oral history included references to George Washington as Ford's father. The media responded with typical enthusiasm. All of a sudden, for the first time, Washington was being portrayed to the general public as an unfaithful husband and an uncaring slaveowner.

Scholars at Mount Vernon conducted a detailed review of the archives in search of documentation that would suggest the alleged relationship between Washington and Ford's mother, a slave named Venus, who belonged to Washington's brother, John Augustine Washington. Editors at *The Papers of George Washington* — the world's best source of detailed information about Washington's life and travels — were contacted to further extend the investigation.

Washington's brother and his family resided at Bushfield, which is some 95 miles southwest of Mount Vernon by road. There is no documentary evidence that Washington visited Bushfield during the period when Venus would have conceived her son. In fact, there exists absolutely no evidence that Washington and Venus ever met each other.

West Ford did indeed become a very important figure on the Mount Vernon stage, but he moved to Washington's estate in 1802 with Bushrod Washington, three years after George Washington's death. He received his freedom in 1805, worked at Mount Vernon in a number of jobs, and provided advice to the Association during the earliest years of the restoration. He is thought to be buried in the slave burial ground.

It is likely that the parentage of West Ford will not be the last question to arise about Washington's relationship with specific slaves. There are those who believe that the recent revelations about Thomas Jefferson and other plantation owners prove that "they all did it." But there are many more people who feel that consistency was an important hallmark of Washington's life, and that his good judgment and character did not desert him in his personal relationships with slaves.

A more frequent question asked by visitors to Mount Vernon is why Washington did not free his slaves sooner, or why as president, he failed to address the issue of slavery. There is no pat answer. Washington's beliefs and feelings about slavery changed dramatically during his lifetime. He inherited his first slaves at age 11, and as a young plantation owner, he accepted slavery as an essential part of managing the business of a southern plantation. But his experiences in the Revolutionary War seem to have transformed Washington's opinion about slavery. In 1786 he wrote to Robert Harris, saying "there is not a man living who wishes more sincerely than I do, to see a plan adopted for the abolition" of slavery.[26] Yet as president, he recognized the volatility of the issue and judged that any attempt to eliminate slavery would destroy the already fragile Union. After solving so many other problems, President Washington avoided the issue of slavery entirely.

At each year's Slave Memorial ceremony, a special wreath with nosegays representing participating organizations is placed at the memorial.

Poet and professor Nikki Giovanni from Virginia Tech has participated in several of the annual wreathlaying ceremonies at the Slave Memorial.

But when he returned to Mount Vernon, he drafted a will that provided freedom to his slaves upon the death of his wife. He set aside funds to take care of those who could not care for themselves.[27] By dissolving Mount Vernon's labor force, Washington knew that the plantation he worked 40 years to create would never survive intact.

Nine presidents owned slaves, but only one set them free. Washington knew that his every action was watched by the nation, and there is no doubt that he hoped others would follow his lead.

The Association has solicited the advice of outside scholars and educators in an effort to provide balanced answers to these questions. In doing so, the Association established a network of close contacts in the field. Still, it was not until 1990, when Mount Vernon joined forces with a new group called Black Women United for Action, that the Association found a way to truly connect with the surrounding community.

Sheila Bryant Coates, the founding president of Black Women United for Action, approached Mount Vernon with a new idea. She felt strongly that the Slave Memorial at Mount Vernon, still thought to be the only memorial to 18th-century slaves in America, had the potential to be the inspiration for an annual event and ongoing educational programs.

The official program for the inaugural event, held on September 22, 1990, included this explanation:

Black Women United for Action, in researching a major project focusing on the contributions of African Americans to the history of Fairfax County, became increasingly aware that very few persons in Fairfax County and elsewhere know of the existence of this memorial to slaves. Because there is no other lasting tribute to African-American slaves, whose contributions are an integral part of the history of our nation, Black Women United for Action felt it imperative that national focus be placed on this unique memorial. And so it is that those of us gathered in assembly here cannot help but reflect on the significance of this event occurring in the Commonwealth of Virginia – Virginia, the site of the Mount Vernon estate and the home of the nation's first president; Virginia, to whose shores the first African slaves were brought to America in 1619; Virginia, whose people are the first to elect an African

American as governor, L. Douglas Wilder, the grandson of slaves.[28]

Governor Wilder served as the keynote speaker, addressing the struggles of the past, the recent progress of the present, and the challenges that still exist in the future. Inspirational music was provided by the Hampton University Choir, and an original poem was recited by Sheryl Sims to commemorate the occasion. The wreathlaying that closed the event was a solemn and moving experience.

Reactions to the event were so positive that a special committee was formed to plan a second installment. In an effort to communicate the importance of the Slave Memorial to a new generation, Black Women United created a youth program that culminated with teenagers serving as participants in the program. Additional research on individual slaves enabled the Association to put together a list that included names, ages, family relationships and occupations. At the beginning of each ceremony, these names are recited by junior and senior high school students, with great respect and dignity.

Over the years, the annual commemorations have focused on the Underground Railroad Movement, with special guests from Nova Scotia in Canada, and on the bravery and achievements of the Tuskegee Airmen. With the help of longtime supporter Nikki Giovanni, an award-winning poet and professor at Virginia Tech, a new writing competition was established to encourage young authors to reflect, in the most meaningful and creative way possible, on their links to their heritage.

A number of accomplished leaders from several walks of life have accepted the honor of laying the wreath, including Emmy Award-winning actress Cicely Tyson; Dr. Louis W. Sullivan, former Secretary of Health and Human Services; television journalist Renee Poussaint; and ambassadors from several African nations. The artistic portion of the programs has been equally diverse, ranging from interpretive dance to a traditional "calling the spirit of the ancestors."

Yet the atmosphere of the program is less about ceremony and more about family. Congressmen sit next to babies in arms, and as the event comes to a close at the Memorial itself, each and every

Several hundred people gather around the Slave Memorial at the annual ceremony co-sponsored by Black Women United for Action.

person is a participant. Sprigs of boxwood cut from bushes undoubtedly planted by Washington's slaves some 216 years ago are distributed to one and all for placement at the Memorial. No one has to speak the words engraved on the stone steps — faith, hope, love — to know that these feelings are present.

The annual Slave Memorial ceremony is marked in indelible ink on the calendars of many local families, and for more than a decade, the leadership of Black Women United has made the event among its top priorities. In addition to Sheila Coates, who possesses a vision and energy that is truly contagious, Virginia Williams, Deloris Baskfield, Ruby Banks, Clyde Hunter, Muriel Lites, and so many others have given countless hours to make this day a unique and memorable one on the Mount Vernon estate.

Clearly, the issue of slavery is not just a part of Mount Vernon's past and present, but also its future. Before the end of 2002, a replica of a typical slave cabin will be reconstructed at the George Washington Pioneer Farm site. For the first time, visitors will have an opportunity to see what life was like on one of the outlying farms, where slaves shared tiny structures with earthen floors. This snapshot of the meager existence of a field slave will not be a pretty one. It is especially important that visitors to Mount Vernon recognize that the vast majority of slaves did not reside in the relative comfort of the

Mansion House Farm.

Within the next decade, the Greenhouse/Slave Quarters will experience a major transformation, as modern interiors disappear and the spaces are returned to their original configurations. Once completed, this structure will represent one of the largest and most authentic slave residences from the 18th-century.

The Association's interpretation of slavery, like its interpretation of George Washington himself, is always changing. Scholars are constantly conducting new research, and archaeologists are finding new clues below the earth's surface. It is a certainty that the Mount Vernon experienced by visitors a decade from now will reveal more about Washington and his family, more about the enslaved Americans who also called Mount Vernon home, and more about the interactions between the two.

NOTES

1   "Farewell address of Ann Pamela Cunningham, delivered in absentia at the Council of the Mount Vernon Ladies' Association of the Union," June 1874, Mount Vernon Ladies' Association.

2   Harrison Howell Dodge, *Mount Vernon: Its Owner and Its Story* (Philadelphia: J. B. Lippincott, 1932), 90-98.

3   Ibid., 90.

4   Ibid., 90.

5   Ibid., 91.

6   Ibid., 97.

7   Ibid., 97.

8   Ibid., 97.

9   Ibid., 95.

10   Ibid., 96.

11   Minutes of the Council of the Mount Vernon Ladies' Association of the Union, 1928, Mount Vernon, Virginia, 75.

12   The estimate of 50 interments was determined during a remote sensing survey of the slave graveyard conducted in 1984, and noted in Bruce Bevan's "A Geophysical Survey at Mount Vernon," 1985, Mount Vernon Ladies' Association.

13 Ibid.

14 Ibid.

15 Minutes of the Council of the Mount Vernon Ladies' Association of the Union, 1929, 62.

16 Walter M. Macomber, "The Rebuilding of the Greenhouse Quarters," *Annual Report of the Mount Vernon Ladies' Association* (1952), 19.

17 Ibid., 26.

18 "The West Quarter," *Annual Report of the Mount Vernon Ladies' Association* (1962), 24.

19 Ibid., 25.

20 Athena Papamichael, *Slave Burial Grounds at Mount Vernon: Towards Inclusion*, George Washington University, December 8, 1989, 9.

21 Dorothy Gilliam, "Remembrance," *Washington Post*, February 26, 1982, B1, and "Memorial," *Washington Post*, February 28, 1983, D1.

22 Ibid.

23 Athena Papamichael, *Slave Burial Grounds at Mount Vernon: Towards Inclusion*, 15.

24 Donald M. Sweig, "A New Mount Vernon Memorial: Dedicated to More Than Washington's Slaves", *Fairfax Chronicles*, Vol. VII, Nov. 4, Nov. 1983-Jan.1984, 2.

25 Ronald L. Chase, The Gum Springs Historical Society, "Commemorative Program for the 125th Anniversary of Bethlehem Baptist Church," .

26 George Washington to Robert Morris, April 12, 1786, *The Writings of George Washington from the Original Manuscript Sources, 1745-1799*, ed. John C. Fitzpatrick, 39 vols. (Washington, D. C.: U.S. Govt. Print. Off., 1931-44), 28: 408.

27 *The Last Will and Testament of George Washington*, edited by John C. Fitzpatrick, 5th ed. (Mount Vernon, Va.: Mount Vernon Ladies' Association, 1982).

28 Official Program, A Ceremony Commemorating The Slave Memorial at Mount Vernon, September 22, 1990. Mount Vernon Ladies' Association.

PHILIP J. SCHWARZ, Ph.D., is a Professor of History at the Virginia Commonwealth University in Richmond, Virginia. He is the author of numerous works on slavery in Virginia, with his most recent book entitled, *Migrants Against Slavery: Virginians and the Nation*. Professor Schwarz has served for seven years as director of the Stratford Hall Plantation Seminar on Slavery for history and social studies teachers and museum educators.

JEAN B. LEE, Ph.D., is a Professor in the Department of History at the University of Wisconsin, Madison. Her forthcoming book, entitled, *Mount Vernon and the Nation: From the Revolution to the Civil War*, is scheduled for publication by W. W. Norton and Company. Professor Lee serves as a member of Mount Vernon's Advisory Council of George Washington Scholars.

LORENA S. WALSH, Ph.D., is a Senior Historian with the Colonial Williamsburg Foundation, in Williamsburg, Virginia. She is the author of a number of prize-winning books, the most recent of which is, *From Calabar to Carter's Grove: The History of a Virginia Slave Community*. Dr. Walsh's research findings were instrumental in developing the interpretive plan for the reconstructed quarters at Colonial Williamsburg's Carter's Grove plantation.

MARY V. THOMPSON, M.A., is the Research Specialist in the Mount Vernon Collections Department. The social life of the enslaved people on the Mount Vernon plantation is her particular focus of scholarly interest, and she has lectured widely and published extensively on that topic. Her most recent article is entitled, "'And Procure for Themselves a Few Amenities': The Private Life of George Washington's Slaves," which appeared in *Virginia Cavalcade*.

DENNIS J. POGUE, Ph.D., is an Associate Director of Mount Vernon, with responsibility for overseeing all preservation activities on the estate. He is currently conducting research in preparation for reconstructing a log slave quarter at Mount Vernon. Dr. Pogue's most recent publication is, "The Transformation of America: Georgian Sensibility, Capitalist Conspiracy, or Consumer Revolution?", which appeared in the journal *Historical Archaeology*.

EDNA GREENE MEDFORD, Ph.D., is Associate Professor of History at Howard University, in Washington, DC. She has written and lectured extensively on the broad topic of African-American history, but with a particular emphasis on the study of free people of color in 19th-century America. Professor Medford is the director of the historical component of the New York African Burial Ground Project, and has served as a consultant and featured commentator for C-SPAN on a number of their historical program series.

JAMES C. REES, M.A., is Executive Director of Historic Mount Vernon. During his tenure, he has overseen the development of numerous innovative programs focusing on interpreting the lives of the enslaved people who worked on the plantation. These programs include a daily "Plantation Life" tour, an audio tour focusing on the plantation outbuildings and the activities associated with them, and the annual rededication of the Slave Memorial at Mount Vernon.